ONYEKA NWELUE

ONKEA TWELUE

ONYEKA NWELUE
A TROUBLED LIFE

M.M OKORIE

Abibiman
Publishing

New York & London

First published in Great Britain in 2022
by Abibiman Publishing
www.abibimanpublishing.com

Copyright © 2022 by M.M Okorie

Abibiman Publishing is registered under Hudics LLC
in the United States and in the United Kingdom.

ISBN: 978-1-9989958-2-0

Cover design by Gabriel Ogunbade

Printed in the United Kingdom by Clays Ltd.

For **Onyeka Nwelue**,
Friend, fighter, survivor.

CONTENTS

Introduction   1

Prologue   3

When Your Best Friend Dreams Of Dying   7

Beginnings   31

Ezeoke   37

Leopard In A Literary Jungle   45

Artistes   61

Consolato D'italia   75

African Movie Academy Awards 2016   97

The Documentary   113

Ambassador Ghanashyam   123

The Beating   135

The Lake   147

Dreams May Come True But Never Free   159

Ezeoke To Oxford   173

Gallery   179

Glossary   191

INTRODUCTION

THE TOUR DE FORCE CALLED ONYEKA NWELUE
Onyeka Onwenu

Onyeka Nwelue sought me out and introduced himself to me, with a copy of his first book, "The Abyssinian Boy".

He was a bold, self-assured young writer and a whole lot more. This was in 2009.

It has been interesting to watch him develop into a vibrant voice, through his books, films, musical interests on what is authentic African creativity. His creative instincts derive from his deeply rooted connections to his home and general environment. With that connectedness, Nwelue offers the world the best of what makes him an African and a black man.

I admire Onyeka's zeal for all good things African, his tenacity, persistence and courage in pursuing his dreams, in spite of having to contend with the numerous challenges that confront Africa's creative community, which is lack of support mainly. But Nwelue has never let impediments stop him, as he whizzes around the world, connecting, producing and touching people with his work and promotions. Sometimes all I see of him are the sashaying tails of his long and colorful African attire, the various bindings of his long and matted *dada*[1](hair), as he comes in and out of view.

Part of Onyeka Nwelue's charm is his originality of thought and his passion for life, the idea that you can be yourself, do good and spread love in the world because you are in it.

It is said that when a young person washes their hands well, they can dine with the elders. Onyeka Nwelue has been dining with elders since childhood. Long may he live!

---

1   Dreadlock coiffure

PROLOGUE

When I met Onyeka Nwelue in 2015, I knew I wanted to write about him. I first learned of him in 2013 when his rebuttal to the Nollywood actress – Tonto Dikeh – roused a social media fray. Tonto Dike had declared that there was 'no chance in hell' that she would marry a 'nosy' Igbo man. Onyeka promptly took upon himself the task of returning the insult. His intervention on Facebook caused what appeared an endless row. It was whilst that controversy raged that I connected with him on Facebook.

At our very first meeting, however, he spoke repeatedly of the likelihood of his imminent demise. As we chatted about our dreams and goals, the obstacles to our aspirations as young Nigerians, remarks about his mortality continually surfaced. He sounded as though he wished to compress eternity into a single day, for fear that he would not be alive for much longer. Consequently, I went home that evening pondering this character who elicited curiosity and excitement in equal measure. I thought initially that his disposition was that of a man whom, perhaps, not so pleased with life, was attempting to wrap himself with the bandage of mystery. However, as our acquaintance deepened, that notion was dispelled. I realised that his frequently expressed expectation of a short lifespan was psychologically entrenched and organically self-reinforcing. Wherever that came from, I couldn't tell and I did not want to ask. It was enough for me to know that this was a genuine fear, and that his frequent references to it did not make it any less real for him. So, as our bond grew closer and I became at some point, a part and parcel of his daily activities, I picked up the pen in my mind's desk and began to take mental notes of his life. If this 26-year-old, I said to myself, is so sure he won't make it to 30, I wish to salvage some of the intricate and intimate details of his life as memento for the next generation. Of course, in hindsight, I concede that it was an arrogant assumption on my part to believe I'd have no scrap with death myself.

Onyeka was a bit of a pop-star in the local literary circle, helped in no small measure by his many controversies and his sometimes prima-donna attitude. He had a large social media following, where he extolled friends and bludgeoned foes. He moaned a lot also, mainly, as I suspect, because he was often thinking out loud. He said what most people could only manage in hushed tones and unseen social media DMs. He called out a great deal of people, some of them super celebrities – and they saw it. He lost friends as quickly as he made new ones. He annoyed many, but he entertained many also. For a while, it felt like he enjoyed the controversies he courted, but there were also moments where he endured the strain of those rifts with clenched teeth.

This book, therefore, attempts to make sense of a life that had been marked by peculiar contradictions. It is not a biography of Onyeka Nwelue, nor is it intended to be one. It is merely an attempt to bring to the fore, a nuanced perspective of a life that is so often misunderstood if not hurriedly and unfairly vilified. My intention was to capture the unseen side (or what the Nigerian Afro-beats artist, Naira Marley, may refer to as the 'inside life') of a young Nigerian writer as I came to see it.

The writing had been kept secret to the subject until it was near completion. This was to ensure that all events were captured in their natural state and with the spontaneity of everyday life. The near-finished work was nevertheless presented to Onyeka to ensure that some of the events recorded were not misrepresented. Because real names were captured and events concerning real people were documented, care needed to be taken to redact certain identities where necessary, so as to protect those who needed protection. The work should, therefore, not be read as a comprehensive study of the subject, though it intends to paint a convincing portrait of his embattled life.

Still, while I recognise the need to remain faithful to the facts, a writer is often confronted with many facts. I have, therefore, taken liberty to interpret the many facts at my disposal to the best of my ability. In the biography of J.M. Coetzee by J.C. Kannemeyer, the writer noted that it is not the aim of the artist to reproduce reality faithfully, but to simply process reality. Hence, through ordering and selecting, the artist arrives at a more complete truth than the historian who is bound by facts.

When, in January 2018, I was walking Onyeka to the car at the end of his 30th Birthday Ceremony in Abuja, he made a confession that startled me, but a truth I could've learned about four years earlier if I were interested. He told me he had defied the doctors. I asked, "How? What? Which doctors?" And he replied, "The doctors in India who operated on me in 2014 told me that I will not make it to 30 given the state of my ectopic kidney." It then dawned on me why he had thrown such a lavish party to celebrate himself, and why he had driven his life like a car-racer on wet asphalt. From this confession, several details and events of his life began to add up. Several decisions he made began to make sense to me, and several risks he took did not seem so foolish anymore. In any case, if there is one thing Onyeka's life revealed to me, it is that nothing is ever one thing. He embodied the reality that a life that looks glamourous to outsiders can be fraught with quiet pain. That sometimes, the road to a life of high ambition courses through the tunnel of high drama and heartache. And that you cannot choose one without the other.

Mitterand Okorie
23 November, 2019

I

WHEN YOUR BEST FRIEND DREAMS OF DYING

On 18th February 2018, Onyeka Nwelue sent me a message about wanting to take his life. 'I want to end it. I don't want to continue like this,' he wrote. It would not be the first time I had known him to be suicidal. It was, however, the first time that disposition of his had jolted me to the edge of my seat, because there was something different about that occasion. He had just plunged, headlong, into a morass of trauma.

Before then, I had associated closely with him for about four years, in which I had seen him pass through countless tribulations. However, in the weeks leading to the day of that message, I had never seen a life careen about so fast. How could you celebrate your 30th birthday in the company of Nigeria's loftiest diplomatic representatives, with Oby Ezekwesili on your left,

7

Onyeka Onwenu on your right, Mr. Symington, the U.S Ambassador to Nigeria behind you, in a hall thronged with people cheering in all the languages of Africa, and then suffer a ghastly car accident the following day, be bundled away to South Africa, unable to stand on your feet, condemned to back-shattering pain?

I have read about life giving people 'beat-downs.' I tell you, I have. I have seen great men undone by life's precarious twists of fate, but I had never seen a life hurtle along that fast for anyone I had been close to. Escaping Nigeria's nightmarish health sector for South Africa, my friend Onyeka found decent healthcare in South Africa, which cost the proverbial arm and leg. If a visitor to South Africa does not have health insurance, severe afflictions could leave the indisposed hanging on a volatile thread. Consequently, in a matter of days, Onyeka was obliged to seek funds online for his medical bills. He had been widely and erroneously considered affluent by many who did not know that he seldom bought his own plane tickets for his many international travels. For many, however – particularly young people – this was the time to taunt a haughty man whom fate had dealt a crushing blow, making him sprawl in dust. Gloat they did! From those who termed Onyeka a fraudster, to those who said he had no right to seek Nigerian money if he did not wish to be treated in Nigeria, and those who said he was not entitled to the money of Christians since he was a self-professed voodooist, the dominant public reaction to his plea for help was that he should go and fuck himself.

On my part, I was barely keeping up with the drama, as this was a period of intense work and travel. The United Nation's Secretary General's Envoy on Youth, Ms. Jayathma Wickramanayake, was on her first Africa Mission, and I had just been contracted by the United Nations Population Fund to be her communications attaché. Our tour was to begin in Senegal, and proceed to Gambia, Ghana, Nigeria and end in South Africa, all within a two-week period. Consequently, I had left my base in Durban for Abuja on 30th January to attend Onyeka's 30th birthday celebration, planning to proceed to Dakar on 1st February to receive the UN Youth Envoy at the start of her Africa Mission.

On the evening that I landed in Abuja, I hastened to the venue of Onyeka's book event at the NAF Conference Centre, Abuja. It was a pre-launch get-together organised for him by the Indian Embassy in Abuja. I arrived in company of our mutual friend, Gabriel, who immediately perceived that something was amiss: 'Mitterand, something tells me Onyeka is in some kind of trouble.' Gabriel has a military background, and it turned out that his hunch was right. Onyeka was surrounded by a handful of policemen in plain clothes right after the launch. Not wanting to be embarrassed in front of his Indian diplomatic friends, he quietly lowered himself into the backseat of their waiting car. Gabriel and I quickly got into our own car and followed closely, treading every path, taking every bend until we arrived at the Garki Area 11 Police Station.

That night, Onyeka slept behind the counter, visibly terrified by the probability of spending his 30th birthday in a prison cell, away from his planned party, his guests, his friends, and his book *The Beginning of Everything Colourful*. So intense was his terror that sweat was all over his face. I saw the despair of a man who was sure his enemies had him where they wanted him. Nothing could be grimmer than the dingy, dark halls of the Nigerian Police Force. The legendary musician, Onyeka Onwenu, who had agreed to anchor the birthday event, was now in Abuja. The U.S Ambassador, Mr. Symington had sent an email confirming that he and his wife would honour the invitation. Various dignitaries had done the same. Were they all suddenly going to turn up in an empty hall, with no cake, no sound and no celebrant? Would the food and drinks, hall and music, all paid for, be wasted while the celebrant languished in jail? The prospect was dreadful, yet time was ticking.

At the Police station, we pleaded his case and tried to effect his release. The police remained adamant. While we persisted, we were told that the station was closed for the day, that the DPO had left, and there was nothing that could be done until the next day. Clearly, those that picked him up, because Onyeka owing them huge sums of money, had planned the arrest to be a night affair and this was clearly for two reasons: to ensure that he spent the night in custody, and to use his birthday and book launch event as a bargaining chip to compel his cooperation. Ebuka "Jack-sparrow" Ifeanyi, one of

Onyeka's closest friends and a member of the force himself, made frantic calls that evening but to no avail. By 2am the next morning, when it was clear all entreaties had failed, Gabriel and I went home. "Call Charley Boy and call Jaffey" were Onyeka's last words to us. Jaffey Nwelue was his elder brother. Jaffey could do the most desperate things to get Onyeka out of trouble, and on his part, Onyeka only sought his help in desperate situations. Charley Boy is a charismatic man, whose presence the police, and in fact, a great many people in authority, would respect. I have seen that happen a few times. Onyeka was clearly at his wits' end, and those two were his trump card to an early exit, or any exit at all from those dreadful prison walls.

Charley Boy groaned under the weight of his interrupted sleep when he picked up my call. However, and although only half-awake, he promised to come for Onyeka the following day. He mentioned that he was already billed for the 7am flight from Owerri to Abuja that morning, and would come straight to the police station on arrival. At about 6am, Gabriel and I had hurried back to the police station. There, we met other friends of Onyeka's who had congregated at the gate, spending the night there. They had defied the orders of the Police to vacate the premises and denied themselves the comfort of a warm night rest. Charley Boy made good his word and was at the police station by 10am, sauntering into the DPO's office with a poise and resolve that convinced everyone that Onyeka was coming home. Onyeka told me later that the DPO, a tall, light-skinned lady, was so star-struck that she was keener on having a long, aimless conversation with Charley than on discussing his release.

The clock continued to countdown really fast between when his creditors would be sufficiently pacified to drop the case, and when the police would close the books on it. The police, however, true to form, were at their racketeering best—agreeing to close the case, first with 20,000 naira, then requesting another 50,000 naira after the first amount was paid. It was the sort of subaltern shadiness that made one resolve never to have anything to do with them. Those who believe they've fallen prey to bait-and-switch scammers in life must pray never to meet the Nigerian police.

By the time Onyeka was finally released, he had only two hours to get down to his hotel, get dressed and make sure all arrangements would proceed as planned. The first person he called was Onyeka Onwenu, who had left Lagos the previous evening to attend the event, but had found the celebrant's number switched off. Onyeka would have wriggled out of that police net earlier if he had called her, as some of us advised him to do, but it was not the sort of place he wanted 'Mummy' (as he called her) to see him in. He appeared always careful, even determined, not to plague his most cherished friends with his personal problems. 'If what you often bring to them is your burden, they'll be scared,' he would say, 'and you'll chase them away.'

R-L: Oby Ezekwesili, Onyeka Nwelue and Onyeka Onwenu at Onyeka Nwelue@30 celebrations. Thought Pyramid, Abuja. 31 Jan. 2018.

Onyeka Nwelue and Fmr. U.S Ambassador to Nigeria, Stuart Symington during Onyeka @30 celebration

At the Thought Pyramid Centre in Wuse II, the birthday and book launch celebration kicked off in grand style, compèred by Onyeka's uncle, Mr. Bright Nwelue. Artworks adorned the walls. There was a huge backdrop: the banner – *Onyeka at 30* boldly inscribed on it – that riveted everyone entering the hall at the top of the stairs. I had arrived almost an hour late to the thronged hall, but as the night's events progressed, I could tell that while the hall teemed with humans, there was a paucity of gifts. Onyeka did not mind though, as he smiled in all the languages of Africa. Thirty meant something. A great deal. That milestone of three decades was a personal triumph over the prognoses that death would sweep him into the afterlife at a young age. It was a personal victory over the fragility of health. A conquest lap over a doomed prophesy of death that was supposed to arrive through the cracks of an ectopic kidney which doctors in India had predicted would not see him live to be 30. Suddenly, 30 meant in some sense that he would now live forever, having overcome his own frailty and the morbid fear of being reminded of how short a lifespan he would have. This was the beginning of everything colourful. Or so he thought!

It was astonishing that only hours later, the rainbow colours of celebration turned a catastrophic black. A Toyota Tundra SUV smashed into Onyeka's car, right on the side of the backseat where he was sitting. The impact was shattering, smashing into his pelvic bone and rendering him immobile.

This marked, for him, a descent into the depths of depression. It was a terrifying epiphany too. Nearly every friend he knew kept their distance. Some acted from shame that they could not help, others out of concealed spite. Either way, they gave neither financial assistance nor emotional support. For a 'people's person', which he considered himself to be, Onyeka was severely hurt, if not crushed by this. The dismay must have deepened the trauma of his misfortune. There is nothing worse than thinking you have friends, only to realize they are not that into you.

On social media, Facebook in particular, where he and his polemics were most popular, he was taking a battering. He was being called a scammer who was using a minor accident as a decoy to extort money from the public. True, he shamed Nigeria regularly on his page, condemning it as a hellhole of scavengers where everyone was sweaty and smelled of *moi-moi*.[2] By this token, his traducers argued, he must not reap the goodwill of those he had viciously lampooned. Many others openly wished him death, insisting that his present affliction would eventually claim his life.

I landed in South Africa on 11th February, 2018. It was the final destination for the UN Youth Envoy's Africa Mission. On the morning we arrived in Johannesburg, however, we had only two hours to clean and freshen up, before going for the start of the day's events. It had been

---

2   Steamed bean cake.

11 days of gruelling work, report writing on the Envoy's meetings, transcribing recorded audio and video clips, fitting them into news formats, submitting them to the United Nations Information Centre in New York, and basically rinsing and repeating with little sleep and rest in between. It was the same for everyone on the team, including the Envoy herself. The only difference was, it was my first time in such a position, and it seemed that while everyone was running on three batteries, I was struggling to run on one. However, two days later, I managed to heave myself out of bed at 4.30am, and took a long Uber ride from Garden Court Hotel (where I was lodging), to Kensington, where Onyeka was staying.

I handed him a flash disk he had asked me to collect from a man who had subtitled his film *Agwaetiti Obiuto*, from Igbo to English. It was painful to see Onyeka confined to a wheelchair, swollen from immobility and sleeplessness, bingeing on painkillers.

'*Nna*,[3] have you seen all the things young Nigerians are saying about me?'

I nodded, my eyes deliberately averted from his as I gazed at the blank TV screen in the room.

'Why are they acting like I'm holding back their destiny?' he continued. 'And for this, I must make sure I get out of this state. I must get out of this wheelchair so I can wipe out those smiles on their faces.'

This determination failed to conceal the hurt in his

---

3   Literally 'father' but used to address male acquaintances

soul. He smarted not only from the jeers of perceived nonentities gloating over his sorrows, but from the indifference of friends and family. Weeks after his accident, many friends and members of his family were yet to call him on the phone. 'It's like they're waiting for me to die, *Nna*. These are people I did everything for,' he said in grieved tones.

When I left the house for my hotel, I felt unsettled. I struggled to muster the composure to continue the job I had been paid to do. However, on my return to Durban a few days later, I found that Onyeka's mood and psychological health were increasingly deteriorating. His state could be fathomed even from his speech. The strength had ebbed from his voice. He was devoid of humuor or mirth. He sounded like one who was fast losing the will to live.

This was why his *I want to end it all* message roused me to acute apprehension, prompting a silent prayer that he would never venture down that path.

Contrary to the widespread view that suicide is a coward's option, I would consider the act as requiring enormous courage to execute. I feel it is wrong to deem it cowardly in any respect. If there was anything preventing Onyeka from taking his life then, it was not the lack of intent, but the lack of heart to translate intent to action. It is one process to hit rock-bottom, and another to bury oneself alive. Suicide was like burying oneself alive. On my part, I tried to counsel him by making myself available to chat about sundry random happenings, long enough for our discourse to become a veritable distraction. However, I knew, deep down, that when he uttered those words, *I don't want to go on living like this*, it couldn't be likened to his habitual social media rants, nor a hollow presentiment of death. He was bemoaning the broken pieces of his soul. His life was upended by a thousand shrapnels of physical and emotional agony. He was plainly in his darkest hour: his Gethsemane.

I imagined what kind of disaster this must have been for him, even though I do not think I had the ability fully to fathom its gravity. To plummet from the peak of celebrity to the depths of infirmity in less than 24 hours, is dizzying. It is like starring in an unscripted horror movie, only to discover that the events were real and you were the victim of the show. To pass from a roomful of one's heroes and admirers, being acclaimed as an exceptional 30-year-old, to sudden incapacitation, tended like a toddler because you are incapable of standing, let alone walking. To go from the globetrotter apparently traversing continents at a moment's notice to confinement in a body blasted by pain, spending days either lying on your back or pushed about in a wheel chair. This was Onyeka's new reality, a pitch-black night with no silver lining for relief.

Despite this bleakness, I imagined that perhaps his film *Agwaetiti Obiuto* gave Onyeka the impetus to live and carry on. The film had cost him a whopping six million naira. It was part of the reason why he was in debt, hounded by Police and EFCC[4] whenever he landed in Nigeria. In fact, on one of those occasions, he was picked up straight from the Lagos International Airport by the EFCC and detained for one day. Onyeka was only released when the popular blogger, Linda Ikeji, issued a 1.1m naira cheque to defray part of the debt and free him. The Abuja police incident happened only a month after that. These incidents moved me to tell him, when we met in the colourful bustle of the hall at Thought Pyramid, 'Nna, your life is too embattled. Will it always be like this for you now?'

As the flames of Onyeka's ordeal flared on, the ever-dependable Peace Anyiam-Osigwe opened a Facebook message thread. For it, she picked some of those closest to Onyeka to serve both as guided voices soliciting funds on his behalf, and his buffer from the world in his travails. The group included Onyeka's elder sister, Nkechi Nwelue; the famed social media blogger Jon Joi; and Onyeka's close pals – Sola Kuti, Kingsley Aniche and myself. We all strove to provide a bracing shoulder, urging him to have hopes for the fundraising. We advised him to suspend writing and commenting on social media, no matter the provocation. Onyeka asked if he should deactivate his social media account, but we insisted that it should remain, so that the world would not assume we were pulling a trick on humanity. 'Stick around, Onyeka. We need your page to be accessible, but

---

4 Economic And Financial Crimes' Commission

don't speak so you don't throw everything away out of annoyance for things people might be saying about you,' Peace said to him. Sola Kuti opened his official Go Fund Me page and we went to work. However, in over three months, the fundraiser achieved a little over 10 percent of its goal – 1.2 million naira – while the target was 9.6 million. The money had helped shore up his hospital expenses in South Africa, even though he had to stay in a 2-star hotel from where he shuttled to the hospital. If he had accepted a bed in the hospital, all available money would have been spent in under a week. For the uninsured in South Africa, healthcare was terribly costly.

In March 2018, when I returned to Johannesburg to see Onyeka, he was in a new, post-accident phase. He had learnt to cope with his new situation, facing the reality of being physically immobile – at least in the short term. Onyeka was accepting that the pain slicing through his back to his hipbone would be with him for a little longer. I discovered that he kept gin and other liquors by his bedside, obviously within instant reach of his hand. These palliatives he imbibed to numb his pain when the pain killers appeared ineffectual or dilatory. Sometimes, seeing him drink these liquors, I held my breath as he shut his eyes on each gulp. I imagined the burning sensation in his chest as the spirit hit his system. I would watch him subside into sleep minutes later. I often winced in dismay, overcome by a deep pity that I did my best to conceal, for Onyeka hated being pitied.

Besides, by this time, a number of things had changed

about him. Psychologically, he was wriggling free of the trauma that devastated him in the days and weeks immediately after the accident. He was finding his film a source of solace, watching it repeatedly. He had begun to communicate regularly with his diplomatic friends, who assured him that they would give him support through channels permitted to them. The encouragement of the Indian Embassy in Nigeria was an instance. The Embassy informed Onyeka that although it was against their protocol to donate to a private citizen's hospital's treatment, they could intervene by having him treated for free in India. At the same time, another friend in the U.S.A promised to assist Onyeka if he came to the United States for treatment.

Shortly, there were again glimmers of excitement in his life. It was perhaps significant that Teddy-A (Tope Adenibuyan), one of the Big Brother Nigeria contestants, said on live television that Onyeka was his manager, and that he was one of the best in the business of managing artists. Teddy bragged about Onyeka on air, boasting of his links to the Nobel Laureate – Wole Soyinka – and other such powerful quantities who formed a formidable network of associates. Onyeka derived much joy from the many emails he received consequent upon Teddy's acclaim. It appeared to him that for the first time in his dealings with Nigerian artists, Teddy's was one collaboration that he got right, one partner who was eager to give credit to another, openly acknowledging Onyeka's contribution to his increasing success.

That weekend, Onyeka suggested that I accompany him to the Live Eviction Show at the Big Brother Naija House, somewhere in Kensington, Johannesburg. It was the weekend when Leo Da Silva and Ifu Ennada were evicted. At the entrance, all the security men seemed to know Onyeka. Consequently, without any pass, I wheeled him into the venue, as we were directed to a spot where we could stay without interfering with the cameras or crew. I recall the Show's captivating host, Ebuka Obi-Uchendu, stepping up to where we were seated and exchanging smiles with Onyeka. He then reached for the envelope which held the names of the housemate(s) to be evicted from the house.

Just as Ebuka was about to return to the stage, Onyeka instructed him in merry cheekiness. 'Please, you people should not remove my boy o!'

Caught off-guard by the question, a perplexed Ebuka asked, 'But he's not up for eviction today, is he?'

'I'm just saying, I need him to win that money badly,' Onyeka replied, and it seemed Ebuka understood the joke, and smiled.

After the show, when virtually everyone had left, the legendary DJ Jimmy Jatt came by to have a word with us. Onyeka told him about his accident, and how loath he was to risk being treated in Nigeria. DJ Jimmy Jatt shook his head, relating how his own wife was misdiagnosed many times in Nigeria. Soon, YCee, who had given a wonderful performance that night, joined us. A four-way discussion ensued for about 30 minutes while we awaited our Taxify Cab. The following day, we headed for the Nigerian Consulate in Rivonia, Sandton. Fruitful discussions were held with the Deputy Consular and Culture Attaché who promised that Onyeka's new film would premiere at the Consulate. By this gesture, Onyeka's began to find his life gaining added meaning once more. Optimism and purpose were gradually re-established in his life. Onyeka began to crave fitness, and not only so that he could resume his roving life. He also longed to prove to those who expected him to be dead or dormant, that he was once more active, progressing and triumphant.

There was comfort in Teddy-A's blossoming in the Big Brother House. Tall, handsome, urbane and well-spoken, Teddy-A seemed certain to emerge from the House a superstar with whom the entire country would fall in love. The prospect of managing his career was enticing, and his loyalty was comforting. All these contributed in various ways to uplift Onyeka, fuelling his zest for life even as he spent more of every day lying on his bed and watching television.

However, all other cheering factors paled beside Onyeka's regular email exchanges with Wole Soyinka. 'His messages give me life,' he once declared. He showed me some of those messages. Sometimes, not satisfied that I had read them with sufficient absorption, or doubtful perhaps that I might not have grasped the context in which the email was written, he would read it aloud, twinkle in excitement, close the phone and guffaw. 'I hope he knows what these emails do to me. This man is a god. God!'

It must be said, however, that despite Onyeka's dogged struggle to rise from the trauma of the accident, the toxic residue of that crash still chafed his soul. His situation prompted analogy with a man riddled with gun wounds from a failed assassination attempt. The bullets might have been excised, yet the bullet holes remained as eternal reminders of the shock and agony of the attack. However strong the resolve to rise from sorrow and dormancy, those holes continually hurt and depressed. Life for such a man could never, in popular parlance, 'be the same again.'

'Why are people saying all these things about me?' he once asked me, in very sombre and slightly agitated tones. 'Is this how I was hated?' To be fair, Onyeka already knew that he was not widely loved; he just did not know how hated he was. '*Nna*, all the people I stuck my neck out for, all these boys whose problems I would do anything to solve, where are they?' he continued, each question, each line, laced with throbbing emotion. 'You know what? I think I am happy this happened to me. I have learnt.'

And just when I thought he had emptied all the hurt in his chest, he went on an even longer tirade. 'I've had an epiphany. Nna, I poured my goodwill down a rabbit hole. How many of these boys came for me while I was down? Now they recall I can solve their problems because somehow I've managed to stay alive. Because I'm not dead. But they were all waiting to hear that Onyeka Nwelue was dead. Bastards! You know, I used to feel remorse, a bit of hurt when I couldn't help people, the ones who are close to me, but after what happened, seeing how they all withdrew from me, I just tell them off. I just tell people off these days without the slightest care. I feel nothing, *Nna*. I'm even happy to tell them to go fuck themselves.'

Initially, I thought he sounded a bit over-entitled to the kindness of others, until I began to recall the lengths to which he normally went to assist the people he called his friends. Onyeka gave generously, financing drinking sprees in gardens or beer parlours, the drinks on many occasions served with the delicacies smoked fish or pepper-soup. Numerous young men who called themselves Onyeka's friends buzzed around him like bees on honey, hoping to prosper through his contacts, his counsel or his cash. They looked up to him to pave their way, to use his bridges and network to reach their goals. So, when he talked of having been there for people, I understood exactly what he meant. If you needed a Visa to a country that had repeatedly denied your application, Onyeka was the person who would take you to the Plenipotentiary of the country, or the Consular Officer of that country, and convince them that you were a genuinely talented creative who should be trusted. If you were hoping to excel in your writing career, he would be the first to speak to his big writer friends to give you a blurb, to advise you over finding an agent, or to promote your work. If you were an artiste struggling to make headway, he would be the first to get you a decent performance gig, and introduce you to the big boys in the industry with whom he was acquainted. In my own case, for instance, he once introduced me to a contact who worked for an international organisation. This person would give me my first international consultancy contract. Onyeka introduced me to the then Italian High Commissioner in Lagos, Mr. Andrea Pompamaier, with whom I developed quite a cordial relationship, and by the time of his departure, I was introduced to his successor. Those relationships prove effective in the most unexpected ways. I recall vividly how he connected me to the maverick writer, Chigozie Obioma, who not only became a good friend but gave me some of the most memorable pieces of writing advice I had ever received.

Perhaps I shall pause here to cite a rare instance of what it meant to be someone Onyeka cared about, and he cared a great deal for many. In June 2016, under bizarre circumstances, I missed my Turkish Airline flight from Rome to Istanbul, which would connect to the Lagos inbound flight. There had been a bombing at Istanbul Airport the previous evening, and perhaps for that reason, the notice board at Fiumicino airport kept showing 'flight delayed', while the aircraft was already airborne. When I finally made it to the gate, the chip of the boarding pass was no longer active. My frantic hitting of the barcode of my ticket on the chip of the gate did not help, and I knew I was in deep trouble.

At the Turkish Airline counter, the news was conveyed to me that I had missed the flight. I let out a scream so piercing that the entire hall must have heard me. 'Your name was being announced repeatedly, Sir. It's not our fault. Please go and pick up your luggage from the exit wing of the Airport', the customer service lady told me in an utterly unconcerned tone. At that moment, of course, it was as though I had been concussed by a heavy object, and the world became a blurry mass.

The real problem was that having spent the entire night gallivanting through various nightclubs in Rome, enjoying the final moments of my holiday, I had exhausted all the cash on me. In truth, there had been no need for money as I should have been airborne. Now, sunk in dejection, I shuffled to a seat, pondering my life, wondering how I would survive the impasse. Nigeria's Central Bank international withdrawal limit had not helped, as I could only withdraw 50 Euros per day. My *No Show* penalty was 285 Euros. In that moment of utter despair, Onyeka's message popped up on my phone, asking: '*Nna*, where are you?'

'I'm at the airport in Rome,' I moaned. 'I missed my flight. I'm out of cash, one day only left on my Visa. If I don't leave here tomorrow morning, I'll be an illegal immigrant.'

'Calm down', he soothed. 'Send me the reference

number on your e-ticket.' I did. He promptly sent a message: 'Seen it. Hold for 30 minutes. Don't leave the airport yet.'

In less than 15 minutes, the customer service lady signalled that I come forward. She briskly instructed me: 'This is your new ticket. Check-in starts at 5 AM tomorrow. Please be here on time.'

I was almost in tears. Two hundred and eighty-five Euros (then 114,000 naira), provided in a flash! Months later, however, Onyeka told me: 'I didn't actually have to pay that. The lady in charge of operations for the airline is a good friend. I had her do it without paying a dime.'

That incident accurately portrayed Onyeka's benevolence to those close to him. He would gladly support you when all doors appeared shut. If life had dumped you between the devil and the deep blue sea, he would gladly make himself your third option. He helped you spread your tentacles, paving ways, not to boost his own prosperity, but hopeful that if he opened doors for you, you would be able to solve your own problems without needing him in the future. Onyeka possessed an emancipatory kind of kindness, not the sort that kept you on a leash, nor the kind that demanded subservience for sustenance. It was in the course of my reflections on his unbounded generosity, that I began to understand his shock at being abandoned in his hour of trial. It was distressing to realize that those who had dined with him in joyous times had no real affinity with him. This realization was particularly galling, considering that in most cases all he expected – and failed to receive – was the inquiry 'How are you holding up?' He was not even expecting those neglectful friends to ask, 'How may I send you money?' Their silence appeared interminable.

This realisation, without a doubt, cut into him like a hot knife through butter and scarred his soul. It made him regret ever bearing others' problems as though they were his. He knew he was not the nicest person in the world, but those he stood up for, he supported unreservedly and steadfastly. Was he misguided to have expected, in return, a fraction of the benevolence he had dispensed? 'I poured all my goodwill down a rabbit hole.' Those words bore acute sadness and a feeling of hollowness. It was at this stage that Onyeka proclaimed that save for two or three people, he had no more friends, and had no sympathy for former associates who encountered misfortune. To him, they were devourers and parasites. They could, in Achebean parlance, be likened to the proverbial lizard that ruined its mother's funeral.

On my part, it was bewildering and sometimes overwhelming to be witness to, and part of, Onyeka's life. I had a continual courtside view of the audacity with which he lived his dreams, and the turbulence that characterized his path. It is nerve-wracking to watch your close friend's life crash, tumbling from hilltop to pit. Onyeka's life provided the most vivid picture I had ever seen of the fragility of life and all that we call success. You could wake up one morning and find that everything you ever worked for would mean nothing to you if you lost your mental health. You could find that the friends you had spent your life's savings feting and protecting had no love or interest in you. It would wound you, however tough a heart you had. Life could always give you a surprise that could annihilate you, unless you manage by steely resolution to retain your equanimity.

Truth be told, to be friends with a man whose life was continually punctuated by personal troubles and public controversies was to frequently ask oneself the questions: *Why bother? Why am I still here? Why am I still standing with this guy?* I have sometimes borne these questions, wondering if Onyeka would somehow become a 'normal' person, that friend to whom you could just chat over wine or whisky, share life's knowledge and nuggets, and watch the years quietly roll by. However, I was also moved to feel that to entertain these thoughts was to ignore the fact that the trials and troubles that trailed Onyeka's life did not come because he loved them. They came because he was on a quest for greatness, seeking a name that would echo fame and substance. In pursuing greatness in the most unorthodox way, Onyeka, perhaps, created the demons he would spend the rest of his life battling.

2

BEGINNINGS

O n 26th February 2015, I met Onyeka for the first time. It was at Cafe 24, now defunct, then owned by his cousin, Kaka Njoku. It was a wonderful sports bar, with a panoramic view of Abuja from the upper floor where we sat. Onyeka was much taller than I had imagined, but he was the cheerful and chatty character that he was on social media.

Before we got into any serious discussion, he gave me an autographed copy of his third book, *Hip Hop is Only for Children*, which incidentally would win the Nigerian Writers Award for Non-Fiction the following year.

'Thanks for writing that chapter', he said, referring to my contribution to the book. 'It looked like it was one of the most controversial parts of the book,' he added.

'And I know how much you love controversy,' I replied. We both laughed. I had written about Phyno and Splash's use of figurative Igbo in their music, and argued that Phyno's lyrical prowess drew heavily from a street and figurative dialect of Igbo that was popularized in the city of Aba. I recalled his posting an excerpt of this write-up on his Facebook page, kindling a fiery debate that flamed for weeks.

'Forget those idiots,' Onyeka raged. 'They said you were not telling the truth, and I ask: "What is truth?" And why can't we all hold on to our own truths and stop disturbing others? Anyway, I like the interest your work generated.'

In the conversation that ensued, I struggled to keep pace, appraising as many aspects of him as I could. His life and appearance manifested enough contradictions and eccentricities to sustain a week-long theatre play.

'You know, we need to go to Mexico, we have to travel the world, promote, tour, sell books, and engage in a thousand and one ventures together,' he enthused. He had made that suggestion in an email a few weeks before our first meeting.

It didn't matter that we were only just meeting. We bonded fast and conversed with the familiarity of old-time buddies. When I saw that the time was a few minutes to midnight, I asked Onyeka if we could have breakfast together before I headed to the Airport to fly to Tanzania the next day.

'When is your flight?' he inquired.

'1 pm.'

'So you need to be there at least by 10 or 11am.'

'I'll just have to come early to your hotel. I'll make it in time all the same,' I told him. Onyeka cautioned: 'Don't miss your flight, please. There will be many other times.' He suddenly asked, 'And can you do me a favour?'

'What?' I asked, my brows inverted in curiosity.

'Take lots of pictures, in Ethiopia, in Dar es Salaam, in Zanzibar. Everywhere you visit, take pictures. Share them on Facebook as recklessly as you can.'

By the evening of the next day, I was stunned by the reaction to a Facebook post of mine. Due to delays at the Abuja International Airport, the Ethiopian Airlines flight had left 3 hours late. For this reason, I and a handful of others missed our connecting flights, and were, to our delighted surprise, lodged at the Hilton Honours in Addis Ababa for the night. Excited, I took a picture of my steaming dinner which was wheeled into the room on a trolley. On waking up the next morning, I had received about five different messages desperately requesting my financial assistance.

'*Nna*,' I asked Onyeka in an email, 'are these the things you put up with on these frequent travels you live out in front of us?'

'Hahahaha! They were asking you for money, right?'I affirmed, slightly amused as well.

'Nigerians! So predictable,' he replied, laughing even more heartily.

I returned from Tanzania after two weeks, waltzed back into Onyeka's life, and became a witness to some of the milestones of his young life.

One of the first things I discerned about him was his understanding of power and its latent instrumentality. Despite his publicly professed love of money, Onyeka was not nearly as enamoured of money as he was of power. Power – or to be precise, the social capital derivable from being connected to the powerful, especially at the interpersonal level – was what truly dominated his mind. It was, it seemed, his topmost priority. Onyeka believed that money could fail one, but power never did. It was the force that truly flung doors open. He loved the trappings that power allowed a person to possess. Above all, he loved the fact that power could be sought and possessed by those whom accident of birth, or lack of initial privilege, kept far from it. He loved that people of lowly background could influence much so long as people believed they were powerful. Interestingly, he had a similar feeling about fame, especially over how the famous could draw the kindness of strangers, and how they could, by mere uttering of a word, make people hasten to do their bidding.

I recall a certain incident that typified his attitude to power and those who, in any form, possessed it. This was probably on 26th April 2016, at the Transcorp Hilton, Abuja. The Ministry of Information and Culture and the British Council were hosting key figures in Nigeria's creative industries to a conference. At the end of the morning session, when people streamed out for the lunch break, almost everyone wanted to meet and be photographed with Onyeka. The crowd shortly began to move away from him. Where were they heading to? They sought the Afro-pop star, D'Banj. The entire hall wanted a picture of the pop star. Onyeka and I stood and watched the clamour for proximity to a famous man. Onyeka was distinctly displeased, and whispered to me: '*Elekwanu ebe onye nke a si putakwanu ugbu a?*' Meaning, 'From where has this person emerged?'

He continued: 'If this guy hadn't showed up here now, I'd still have been the centre of attention.'

I realized then that having tasted fame, Onyeka would continue to hunger for more. Evidently, he had an arrogant belief in his own greatness, and for this reason, would readily dip his hand in fire if power and fame could be plucked from the furnace. It was also typical of him to take matters in his stride when they did not go as he wished. It was no surprise then that as Onyeka and I stepped into the Hilton Restaurant and found D'Banj having a meal, Onyeka cheekily teased him, "Kai, so fine people like D'Banj dey chop? I swear, if I was fine like you I will not even be eating."

The contradiction, however, was this: Onyeka was a man beset daily with anxiety. Sometimes, this mental condition was intense, and some days, mild. That factor remained in his life, a disturbing force, daily affecting his mood. A social event, an eatery, a conference hall, an unruly concert ground, indeed any crowded setting, could suddenly unnerve Onyeka, impelling him into a quick exit. Trying to contact him then would be futile, for he would be ensconced in the inviolable repose of his hotel room, surfing the world through the wings of the Internet. As he lived only in hotel rooms (at least whenever he was in Nigeria), he could conveniently turn off his phones and remain connected to the world through the hotel Wi-Fi.

In periods of mental strain, Onyeka could shut out anybody, even if they were the President. There was just that urge, so fervent and ferocious to withdraw from the cacophony of society and retreat into solitude. It was as though he must either find a place to be by himself at those moments, or risk utter madness. I recall his parents' wedding anniversary, where a number of people waited to speak to him. Knowing this, and aware of his phobia for crowds, he instructed his then Personal Assistant (PA), a fellow named Fellowship, to fetch his bag from the house. As we walked to where I had parked my car, he urged me to drive off quickly as he could not wait to get away.

This, perhaps, was the first time I realised that Onyeka's relationship with fame was as oppositional as it was self-reinforcing. As a person, it did seem he consciously courted fame and believed in its trappings. On the other hand, he knew – but probably came to that realisation later – that fame could be exhausting and a man who courted it risked losing his peace.

3

EZEOKE

It was 9:45 pm, but Onyeka insisted we must leave Oguta for his village, Ezeoke. 'I'm not a good night-driver,' I pleaded.

'Don't worry, nothing happens to the son of Ogbuide,' he assured me. 'I'll be in the car with you.' The other three people, Oliver, Fellowship, and an actor friend, Sixtus, drove behind us in another car. I was displeased at being compelled to abandon my desire to remain in Oguta and drive to Owerri in the morning. However, I concealed my annoyance from him. I had once flared up in anger before Onyeka, and he accused me of acting like a possessed beast. My eruption had resulted, not from a serious issue, but banter that took an unforeseen turn. Curiously, on the morning of that day, when we met for breakfast, he told me in typical psychic vein that he suspected I had issues with my temper. I laughed it off, saying the spirits had misinformed him on that occasion. By the evening of that very day, in Bolingo Hotels, Abuja, we were in a room with superstar disc jockey, DJ Switch; the artist's manager, Ifeanyi Orazulike; Gabriel Damilare, and the actor Uchemba Williams. Onyeka then made a joke which infuriated me. My mood changed, anger welled up from my belly, and I could feel such pressure in my chest that it seemed about to explode. Everyone noticed my rage. I definitely was not amused.

DJ Switch had asked excitedly what everyone did in Abuja. Uchemba Wlliams was obviously a known actor, her manager, Ifeanyi was the president of a U.S NGO, Onyeka needed no introduction, Gabriel had a stellar career in NGO work and health, and when it was my turn to speak, Onyeka shouted from the other end of the room, 'This one is very brilliant, but he's jobless.'

The entire room broke into laughter. I too could have laughed, but his jest was not funny to me. I had been thinking throughout that week of becoming an industry person. I had wondered what the future held if I failed to get contracted to consult temporarily for some NGO or other. Those were well paid jobs, but fraught with uncertainty. Once one contract was completed, there was no guarantee as to when the next would come. I had become worried about societal acceptance, especially in Abuja where, until you mentioned the establishment where you worked as a salaried worker, no one took you seriously. Consequently, Onyeka's joke had touched a raw nerve.

As my reaction stilled the room, Onyeka said he contemplated leaving, because what was meant as a joke had gone horribly wrong. In return, I had to defuse my anger to save face, and avert the disintegration of what had begun as a merry evening. I began then to try not to lose my temper around Onyeka, who was in fact highly sensitive.

As I prepared, against my wish, to drive from Oguta in the dead of night, he told me: 'I have to buy a goat tonight which will be used for my parents' thanksgiving service in church tomorrow. It would be too late to get it were we to leave Oguta for Ezeoke in the morning.' Without another word, I started the car and we left for his village. On our way, about 3 kilometres before the Maria Assumpta Cathedral in Owerri, my Mercedes crashed into a wide and deep pothole. The smell of burning tyres immediately assailed our nostrils, and I feared the front tyre had been ruptured. My vision had not been very clear, and I was driving at 90 to 100 km an hour. At that speed, I had suddenly seen a wide black hole, which looked at first like the silhouette beneath the car's headlamps, but appeared much wider as the car drew close. It was too late to brake instantly, and too late to swerve away from trouble without crashing against the concrete road demarcation. I applied the brakes gently, and steered cautiously to the left, hoping as much as possible to mitigate the eventual damage. The front tyre on the passenger side crashed into the hole, bending and scarring the wheel drum. Fortunately, as the tyre was tubeless, leakage from the wheel drum did not prevent us from completing the trip.

At St. Paul's Anglican Church, Ezeoke, a church warden, lanky and clad in a brown gabardine suit, impatiently motioned at Onyeka's seat, drawn by Onyeka's bared dreadlocks, irked that some 'woman' had walked into church without covering her head.

'*Biko puo ga kpuchie isi gi*,'[5] he instructed, standing behind Onyeka, without caring to know or see the face in front of the hair. However, as Onyeka turned, the smugness vanished from the warden's face. He saw it was a man, and did not know how to react. Seated three pews behind, I saw Onyeka stare at him with contempt, and he disappeared without another word.

At the end of the service, a crowd quickly gathered around Onyeka. Some of the people just wanted pictures, others to see his hair up-close, and some were there to gossip or confirm a tattle. A number of them wished to assure themselves that it was the Onyeka they knew, son of Sam and Ona Nwelue, born and bred in the village of Ezeoke, who was truly making waves as they had heard. As I stood aside and watched, the gossips were having a field day. Frankly, Onyeka evinced no keenness on hearsay. On that occasion, however, he asked whether

---

5   Please go outside and cover your head.

I had listened to the chatter, and perhaps overheard comments about him.

'They said you are possessed by some big spirit, and that this hair you are carrying isn't for nothing,' I started, relating what I had heard. 'They said you had gone far – that is, that in the occultic realm, you're quite high up the chain of command... I heard someone telling his friend that he heard you were such an avid voodooist that any day you came into a church, you would fall on your face and start convulsing like those people we see on TV, that the Holy Spirit would knock you down... They said you were a walking *ganja*. That you smoke so much weed, you made yourself a smoking pipe so you could easily drug yourself up in the shortest possible time... They said you are now a Professor, and you go all over the world travelling and speaking to large crowds of people... They said the Onyeka that grew up in Ezeoke has become something big and unrecognisable.'

After each 'they said', Onyeka let out a guffaw that made the group listening to our conversation stagger backwards, then reassemble.

Onyeka presently resolved: 'My parents are already home; let's all go home and join the anniversary reception in the house.' The throng dispersed and followed him home.

At the reception, Onyeka proved a cheerful and attentive host, hoisting the camera around and recording all he thought necessary, simultaneously coordinating the event. 'Have you eaten? Have they served you? Please join the picture. Have you taken a picture with them?'Those were his concerned remarks as he moved from one individual to another. 'Them' of course meant the celebrants, his parents.

On that festive and sunny Sunday, Onyeka's mother was aglow, looking too young to have born such a big offspring. She manifested the poise of one who had spent her working years as a teacher and disciplinarian. Friends and well-wishers congratulated her and her husband, many remarking that she still looked well and young. All of Onyeka's siblings were present, except his elder brother Jaffey who was based in Budapest, and his only sister who lived in Delhi. The siblings present all addressed the guests and congratulated their parents.

When it was time for the parents to speak, Onyeka's father spoke first. Although in his sixties, he was brisk and vigorous in both movement and speech. He praised his wife, and called himself unbelievably fortunate to be blessed with the children they had produced and raised together. It was, however, his wife's speech that brought half the company to the brink of tears. Onyeka himself was overcome, and rushed from the scene before he dissolved into tears. The party was held on the terrace of the house. Onyeka made his way inside, and stood there to hear the rest of his mother's address. In the crack of her tone, in the emotion and breaks of her voice, could be discerned a mother's anxiety to establish that, although she had no favourite child, she recognised Onyeka as a special offspring.

'Enwere mgbe ogbajuru doro, o di ka di m ogaghi a la ya. Owukwanu Onyeka nwa m a; o ya kpo anyi ga India, kwuo ugwo ihe n'ile. Chai! Onyeka nwa m, chukwu gozie gi.' [6]

The heartfelt speech was the high point of the event. Perhaps that compliment was the best welcome that Onyeka received in Ezeoke Nsu, a town which held a special place in his heart.

I watched him take countless pictures of the village to gratify his nostalgia for it. He beamed his lens at everything that moved. He photographed palm trees which produced the fresh palm wine that gave him his first taste of alcohol; the stream where he fetched water as a child; the old family farmland; his old primary school, the Community Primary School, Umunuhu Nsu; and the red sand and dusty roads of Ezeoke which no one had bothered to tar. As we drove away, we observed that a strong breeze was blowing. Onyeka rose through the squared open roof of my car, caressing the palms and bamboo trees which flanked the narrow road, causing swishing sounds. I swiftly accelerated,

---

6 At a time of trial, when it appeared my husband might not survive, it was this son of mine, Onyeka who took us to India and paid for everything. *Chai*! My child Onyeka, may God bless you.

and the car's speed was such that Onyeka panicked and laughed, calling me 'Mad boy!' He adjusted his feet on the chair of the passenger seat, his arms on the car's roof supporting him, while he continued to take photographs of the idyllic rural town.

4

LEOPARD IN A LITERARY JUNGLE

In the first paragraph of the only review I ever read about my novel – *All That Was Bright and Ugly* – the reviewer related that he stumbled upon a conversation in which the book was described as 'trash'. Intrigued by that assessment, he decided to read a copy himself. Whilst acknowledging the many editorial flaws in the work, the reviewer applauded the writer (myself), for successfully weaving a love tale that escaped the pitfalls of boredom or monotony. In my opinion, it was a fairly balanced review, perhaps, even slightly entertaining. My mind, however, was riveted on the gossip about me in the appraisal. I strained to imagine where it had all come from, those behind it, what their faces were like, their motivation, how long they might have kept tabs on me, and what I might have done to them. I wondered if the petty gossip was prompted by genuine concern for art, or were merely swipes at an author whose face was not particularly appealing. Initially, these questions preoccupied me, replayed themselves in my subconscious, until I made a conscious effort to jettison them. I understood the gossip to be indicative of the crab mentality which typified many lives in Nigeria. These reflections precede an account of an interview that Onyeka once granted.

It was in December 2015, and the interviewer was an award-winning writer and journalist, Abubakar Adam Ibrahim. I recall Onyeka calling Nigerian writers 'weaklings'. Surely, no assemblage of people or group is free of faults. However, it does feel sometimes that Nigerian writers' communities have elevated backbiting to an art, and fallen into the familiar Nigerian trap of using art as an instrument of 'hustling'. For example, if someone is nominated for an award, other writers swiftly denigrate their work. They would emphasize typographical errors in the work, however minute or debatable they might be. They would swiftly denounce the writing as inept, be scathing over its promotional publicity, and sometimes even express doubt over the book's existence. There is such inexplicable zeal to diminish and destroy other peoples' literary ventures. If the book or piece of writing duly wins an award, a volcano of bile may erupt, forming itself into acrimonious factions, continually solidifying.

There is never a shortage of reasons for hating a writer. Resentment could be roused by being published in the New York Times or The Guardian, or by having more money than your struggling or overlooked colleagues. If you are a generous person, tending to pick up the bills of your colleagues, you should expect that your pearls would shortly be trampled upon, and be blasted by the resentment of recipients of your largesse.

Some Nigerian writers have had this experience. Interestingly, it was in moments and matters of this nature that Onyeka thrived. Then would his loyalty be fierce and unflinching, to the consternation of the lampooning crowd. He would manifest his contrarian disposition, standing by his friends. The world might not always count it a stellar trait, but to Onyeka, his friends are never wrong, and if they were, he would stand with them against social media lynch mobs.

I recall his reaction to the sexual assault allegations against award-winning poet, Chijioke Amu-Nnadi. Amu-Nnadi was someone I admired greatly, although I had never met him. He was generous in sharing his talent, regularly posting his poetry on Facebook. Each piece I read seemed more captivating than the one before it. When the accusations began to tumble down – young ladies saying he hugged them improperly, kissed them on the mouth without their consent, sat them on his lap, and other such complaints of sexual assault – I was dismayed. I could not reconcile my image of the poet with these allegations. As days went by, there always seemed to be yet another girl accusing Amu-Nnadi. I sometimes likened the saga to the #MeToo before the American version appeared!

'It has happened!' Onyeka wrote to me. 'I told you Chijioke was soon going to have problems, the way he threw money around in Nigerian literary circles. I told him this in Uganda where he paid for the flight tickets of a couple of writers to come to the Writivism Festival. People were having a good time and he was picking up the bills. In Frankfurt, he did the same. I even had some writers come up to me to ask what he did for a living. I saw all of this coming. But believe me, Chijioke didn't do any of these things he's been accused of.'

On social media, there were very few people disposed to defend Amu-Nnadi. I am sure there were writers who could argue he was innocent as Onyeka did, but were too watchful of their 'reputation', or too afraid of being mauled by the mob's fury. Onyeka was unhesitating in springing to the poet's defence. His loyalty and resolve in publicly defending Chijioke Amu-Nnadi earned him ferocious denunciation. There were those who spoke of him as a misogynist bereft of soul and morals, an enabler of sexual assaults, and other such slanderous descriptions. I found his insistence on the poet's innocence curious. Even after Amu-Nnadi issued a public apology, acknowledging what he termed as his 'excesses', Onyeka still maintained that he was innocent of the accusations.

On a fine evening about three years later, Onyeka and I were with Amu-Nnadi at Abuja's Hilton Hotel. Amu-Nnadi's account of the nightmarish episode brought me to the brink of tears. The vilification almost wrecked his life. At work, envious colleagues saw it as an opportunity to clamour for his sack. The foundations of his family life were shaken. 'My daughter tried to kill herself and almost succeeded,' he recalled with his head bowed, obviously imagining the tragedy that could have occurred. When he raised his head, he said: 'Thank God there were people who saw her soon after she slit her wrist. If it had been just her in the room and nobody walked in, she would've bled to death.'

Onyeka, livid, threw his hands up in the air, screaming, 'But why did you let everything slide? Why did you issue that apology? I knew those things weren't true. I knew how many writers have asked me what you did and how you made your money. I knew this shit was coming, but no one could try it with me. This is why Charley Boy is my role model. If anyone did it with me, I'd pull the whole house down, and I'd drag everybody down.'

'Well, I didn't write that apology,' Amu-Nnadi explained. 'I wasn't even in the state of mind to comprehend anything, let alone write. Chiedu Ezeanah wrote it and I was happy with it. It was my attempt to quell those riotous attacks on my person and blow out the fire.'

'But they weren't happy,' Onyeka responded. 'I strongly believe that Lola blacklisted me from Ake Festival because I said those girls were not speaking the truth. These people aren't even saints, but they can be so determined in tearing others down.'

As the conversation progressed, I could sense Amu-Nnadi's lingering agony over the entire episode. He spoke of it as though it occurred only the previous night. He recalled every incident, every single girl that wrote and what they wrote, relating what he felt were the real issues: he could no longer finance the frivolous demands they made because they thought he was wealthy. 'One of the young ladies, though,' he explained, mentioning her name, 'I'll admit I had something to do with. But it was totally consensual. I believe she was pressured to line up behind the others to say the things she said.' He would even push himself to the edge of his seat to show me screenshots, chats, and other unsavoury communication from some of those who maligned him. One was a lady who invited him to Lagos, paid for his trip and an additional fee for him to attend a poetry event in Lagos. He showed their back and forth love-struck discourse. After each piece of evidence he relayed, Onyeka would scream: 'Why didn't you put out all of this, so everybody goes down?' I chuckled a few times, but Amu-Nnadi replied that he was happy that he had not reacted in that manner. 'She was married. Despite whatever was done to me, I did not think it was worth destroying anyone's marriage.'

We all reclined on our respective sofas, as though taking time to digest all that had been discussed, or pondering how differently matters would have gone if certain neglected actions had been taken. Onyeka finally broke the silence, saying that he wished certain people had not exaggerated the issue. Pa Ikhide, for instance, was the type of critic who tended to harp so repeatedly on an accusation that everyone would start believing in its veracity. His interventions could be acerbic, though I think, sincerely, never out of malice. He was a powerful literary voice at the time, sending Facebook posts almost every hour, seeking clarification, urging the author Amu Nnadi to come out and clear his name. Calling out folks suspected of wrongdoing is in itself a noble course. It should, however, not be done in a manner that suggests that the accused is guilty of the allegations made against them, or that you are privy to secret information that proves the accused person's guilt.

I recall Ikhide demonstrating similar resentment of the late Pius Adesanmi during the 2015 elections in which he sometimes spoke mockingly of intellectuals who were in bed with Nigeria's hangmen: politicians. Everyone knew of Pius' closeness to El-Rufai (then the Governor of Kaduna State of Nigeria), and other eminent political, diplomatic and religious figures, including Pastor Tunde Bakare. However, considering Pius' history of speaking truth to power, his uncompromising stance towards his own political friends (very few people knew Emir Lamido Sanusi of Kano once sent a private jet to convey Pius from Calabar to Kano, yet he wrote a scathing article criticizing Sanusi's marriage to a girl below 18 years), Pa Ikhide's insinuation was misplaced. Very few people knew that in 2014, Pius Adesanmi rejected a 5-million-naira cash gift from a Niger State politician, who had invited him to give a speech at the opening of a library in the state capital. Considering Adesanmi's local and international stature, it was not unusual for a politician to deem the sum the usual 'thank you for coming' gift. The politician was remorseful, feeling that Adesanmi considered the sum paltry, and asked his aides to double the amount, bringing it to 10 million naira. Pius promptly declined the offer, stating that such a financial consideration was irrelevant to his honouring the invitation to speak. The politician finally pleaded that as he had recently returned with some watches from a trip to Switzerland, he would love to present a timepiece to Pius Adesanmi. It must have been intolerable for a man of Adesanmi's high principles to be accused of giving 'intellectual cover' to his friends in power. That was an instance of how our representation of others and certain issues easily degenerates into disparagement and sometimes breeds longstanding enmity.

I recall Pa Ikhide's book reviews being in that vein. Although they were robust and sensational, they contained objectionable presumptions and assumptions. This tendency made Chigozie Obioma fall out with him. In Obioma's case, Ikhide had insisted that explaining African expressions or anglicizing 'pidgin' for 'white audiences', proved Obioma was writing for the West. At a book reading at the Roving Heights Bookstore in Abuja, however, Obioma explained this practice as evidence of his being a maximalist: one who enjoyed capturing the essence of things or concepts he fancied. Most of the audience in fact were astounded when the author revealed that his book, supposedly written for America, could not find an American publisher, and it was only a small press in Britain which had never published a book that took a chance on it.

Ikhide's review, added to other publications in the Nigerian literary space (particularly an online fray between the author and Brittle Paper, and a few other Nigerians on Twitter) made Obioma suspend any engagements in the country with respect to book readings or attendance at book festivals. I imagine that turning down an invitation to the Ake Festival in 2016 was partly a result of these experiences.

Onyeka, however, was a writer with an unusual disposition. Writers, I believe, long for a writing life where their works earn them wealth, fame, and literary awards. Travel, too, would be expected, considering the book festivals and readings in various parts of the world. They long to be managed by big – or at least successful – literary agencies, who would pave all necessary paths. It would appear that Onyeka wished to belong in that successful and pampered realm, and he seemed for a while to be on the path to attaining it. He was signed by Pontas Agency some months before they brought Chigozie Obioma on board. This was a focused, businesslike agency. Unfortunately, as Onyeka himself would one day muse, he 'just couldn't produce a manuscript that they could publish.'

This situation seemed to have caused a fundamental

change in his attitude towards writing, and the conceptualization of himself as a writer. As someone who already had a successful first book, *The Abyssinian Boy,* and had a large social media following – which was regularly invigorated by controversies – he sought a closer interface between his life and his art. In this vein, his personality reflected his writing life. While the typical writer relied on their writing to kindle curiosity about their character, Onyeka's personality prompted curiosity over what he wrote. In effect, he learnt to use his persona to generate interest in his writing. It is hard to state whether this actually worked, because defining success is usually a subjective activity.

Onyeka, however, once told me of writers whom he admired, and who drew considerable attention to their art by leveraging on their public image. E.L. Nukoya, he said, was a good example. Nukoya is the author of the award-winning book, *Nine Lives*, and a second book, *Baron of Broad Street.* He is rarely seen in the company of writers, but would have music and film celebrities at his book launches. By so doing, he leveraged on his relationship with celebrities to beam the spotlight on his books. It is hard to tell if Onyeka strove consciously to emulate this model. The path he trod, however, was similar to Nukoya's. Pictures of him presenting copies of his books to eminent Nigerians (which photographs he posted on his social media pages), not only drew widespread interest, but also preserved his identity as a writer.

Jude Dibia was another writer whose style Onyeka loved greatly. He said that people like Jude Dibia and Chijioke Amu-Nnadi 'gave writing a swag.' This was because they were men who were well-off in their professional jobs, yet poured their hearts into their art. There is a general tendency (although particularly applicable in Nigeria) to see writers as perpetually impoverished. On many occasions, I found Onyeka decrying this, and the discussion often tended to return to Dibia and Amu-Nnadi. He felt that, given the relative comfort both writers lived in, they contradicted the image of writers as penurious or pitiable. They rather portrayed writing as a dignified undertaking, whose practitioners could contribute to humanity and live in material comfort.

I later learned that Jude Dibia left Nigeria because the country's rabid homophobia robbed him of peace. The situation in Nigeria remains fiercely homophobia. There are no institutional efforts to rid the country of its obsessive abhorrence of gays. In some cases, writers manifest aversion from the works and lifestyles of their queer counterparts.

It was, however, Onyeka's father-and-son relationship with Wole Soyinka that gave him an envied position in the Nigerian writing community. In Nigeria – and probably most places – if people wished you to introduce them to some eminent figure, they would be careful not to be standoffish with you, or to gossip about you. They would strive to be in your good books. As

Soyinka's mentee and protégée, Onyeka would naturally bask in the Nobel Laureate's renown. These factors gave Onyeka a special status, placing him somewhat beyond the reach of malevolent gatekeepers. Bigger writers seeking access to Soyinka normally sought Onyeka to make it happen. He became someone they could not slight, and he knew it. Once, he jokingly told me: 'When Soyinka passes on, I'm finished. I wish he could live forever.' His attachment to Soyinka stems of course from the love the man's steadfastness and kindliness roused in him, rather than what Soyinka's name can do for him. His attachment to Soyinka has lasted a long time. In 2004, Onyeka was a 16-year-old on a night bus from Owerri to Lagos, impelled by the longing to actually see his hero Soyinka. Considering Nigeria's dismal security situation, that 900 kilometre trip was fraught with risks. However, he was intent on seeing the Nobel Laureate. That night, he had nothing but the clothes on his back, and a shameless exuberance for writing. 'Nothing could've stopped me from going to see Wole Soyinka on that day. I read from the papers that he was to be at the National Theatre, Lagos the following day, and I felt that was the only opportunity I might ever have to meet him.' That meeting would become the start of his association with the man.

Onyeka's clout as an author within the Nigerian writing space owes much to his multidimensional approach to the arts. By plunging into several creative realms – film, music, jazz concerts for foreign missions

– Onyeka was able to use each medium to reinforce the other. In other words, he could sell his books at his film screenings or concert grounds. He could sell his films at his book readings. He made each art form impact the other, interspersing in a seamless way. Onyeka's legs, like the tentacles of a morning millipede, straddled diverse spheres of creative undertaking. This ensured that he remained conspicuous and topical. I used to think all of these might have been due to fate, that finding himself in several creative realms might have been sheer happenstance. I soon understood, however, that it had been a deliberate process. Writing is rarely, if ever, a vocation. I once read an interview of Chigozie Obioma's where he remarked that one should not consider writing a vocation, but a gamble! This pronouncement also helped me make sense of Onyeka's approach to the arts. He seems to have decided: 'While I may never be one of the most read writers, I am determined to be the one you're not in a hurry to forget.'

One morning, over coffee in Maboneng Precinct, Johannesburg, he told me that at the age of 18, he went off to India. 'Curiosity led me there. India was one of the places I had visited many times through books.' Living in the slums of India opened myriad vistas in his mind, making him crave contact with more areas of the world. Having experienced that multifarious culture, he was curious to see other places. After winning the Prince Claus Grant, he spent an entire year visiting more than half the capital cities of Europe. His journeying culminated in the publication of his first poetry collection, *Burnt*.

During this period, he also went on separate tours with Europe-based Jazz artists like Asa and Nneka. On a separate occasion, he joined Seun Kuti (son to the Afro Beat legend, Fela Kuti) on a Euro Tour, where, as he told me, he found the inspiration for his third book, *Hip Hop is Only for Children*. The book was a scathing critique of commercial music which dominated Nigeria's air waves, but was scant of aesthetic substance. Some Nigerian artistes, offended by Onyeka's swipe at them (he criticised them for singing trashy songs and brandishing non-existent wealth on social media), sent him threatening messages.

When I asked him if he still felt the book's censorious stance was justified, he insisted that it was. 'The book was controversial. But it was popular as well. Nigerians love hypocrites. Those who don't tell them the truth. If you say things the way I say them, you'll be everybody's enemy: the government, your benefactors, even the people you're fighting for.' He told me that he did not write the book in a bid to make enemies, but only wanted musicians in Nigeria to do better. He wished that they would respect their craft. 'They have to do live performances with a band; the fans deserve that, not having artists miming their songs.'

His love for good music and his respect for musical talent, he told me, was a huge motivation for the book. As an individual and a 'creative', music appealed deeply to his imagination. 'I admired musicians a lot. I tried to record a song once in a studio, and it was woeful. I learnt to admire those who did it well.' He later established a small record label, La Cave Musik, in Paris, and worked with artists. He attended the Prague Film School in 2010 for a different reason. 'I always felt film had the capacity to communicate to a much wider section of the society. You know, many people would never have known of the writer Mario Puzo, if the film, *Godfather*, hadn't been made. So I always felt strongly that films could be a complementary asset to the craft of writing.'

This conviction might be why he made *The House of Nwapa*, a documentary film about Africa's first female novelist, Flora Nwapa. The documentary appraised the personality of Nwapa, her creative talent and fierce independence, through her books and insights of family members, associates and literary critics both in Nigeria and abroad. Onyeka's second film, *Island of Happiness* was an adaption of his sixth published book, bearing the book's title, and set incidentally in Flora Nwapa's hometown, Oguta. The film depicts the lives of unemployed and poverty-stricken young men in the oil producing town, who wait abjectly on the benevolence of their rent-seeking local authorities. In an uncaring social environment where their only sources of release are sex and alcohol, they become bitter and bloodthirsty.

The film, he told me, was a depiction of the things he had observed in the country, especially among many young people he had encountered. 'Every time I was in Nigeria, I had hundreds of young people around me telling me I could help their careers. I mean, I was still trying to help myself, but because I could travel overseas, sometimes on a whim, they believed I could help them. People were buying me those plane tickets. I was still trying to help myself. But I understood that the system had failed them. The Nigerian system had failed all of us. And I tried to use the film to tell that to the world.'

Now with nine books to his credit, there seems an immense energy powering his ink. The likes of *The Lagos Cuban Jazz Club* (Origami Books, 2017), *The Beginning of Everything Colourful* (Paressia Publishers, 2017), *84 Delicious Bottles of Wine for Wole Soyinka* (editor: Origami Books, 2018), *Island of Happiness* (Hattus Books, 2018) *Evening Coffee with Arundhati Roy* (editor: Hattus Books, 2018), *The Spice Bazaar* (Hattus Books, 2018) and *A Country of Extraordinary Ghosts* (Hattus Books, 2018) were all published over a period of two years. Whenever I teased him about publishing too spontaneously, he responded with a refrain that had become very familiar to me: 'What if I die tomorrow?'

5

ARTISTES

It was 21ˢᵗ March 2014. Jaywon and YQ, decent artistes at the time, together with members of their crew, sat waiting for Onyeka at the breakfast lounge of the Grand Ibro Hotel Annex in Abuja. We were notified about them by the intercom at the hotel's reception. Both artistes needed to be in France for a music performance, but had trouble convincing the country's Consulate that they would not abscond into the streets of Europe afterwards. For citizens of Nigeria living in Nigeria, that suspicion routinely blighted Euro-American visa requests.

Show promoter Ozone, of 03 Media, who had in the past been assisted by Onyeka, brought the artistes from Lagos to Abuja. He had told Onyeka that he believed Onyeka's friendship with some officials of the French Consulate in Abuja might ease the path of the artists. They, after all, only longed to perform their music to their fans in Europe and enjoy themselves.

Consequently, the previous night, both artistes had come to where we were having a drink in Wuse II district of Abuja. I was curious to find they had no celebrity affectations or smugness. On the contrary, they were fawning on Onyeka with the characteristic subservience of those desperate for a favour. I never knew that the challenge of obtaining European visas could be so humbling.

When I remarked their obsequiousness to Onyeka, he told me that he was used to it, and that I must not think much of displays of deference. 'This is how they behave when they want something. The moment their visas are out, they won't be picking up your calls again. If there's anything you want from them, now is the only time you can get it. You know, once they need you, they'll be out to do anything, so use them when you can.'

It was no surprise when in the morning I excitedly told Onyeka that we should go and breakfast with Jaywon and YQ, and his response was 'Let's finish what we are doing. They will wait. Nigerians call it packaging, *abi*? Let them wait there for 40 minutes; we are coming.'

That morning at the French Embassy in Maitama, Abuja, matters did not proceed as anticipated. Onyeka was mortified. We had arrived at the place, but rather than wait in line, Onyeka sought to contact his friend, Paul, an attaché at the Embassy. He hoped Paul would expedite the visa process. It was, after all, what friends were for. Paul, however, was at a meeting with the Mission's Plenipotentiary. We learned later that after repeated calls and text messages from Onyeka, he began to fidget in front of his boss. It has sometimes been the case that Onyeka's friends may feel so indebted to him, or obliged to do his bidding, that they are unsettled when unable to grant his request. As an outsider to his relationship with Paul, I am unable to tell why the young man reacted as he did. His distraction, however, was such that the Ambassador stormed out of the meeting to order that Onyeka should leave the premises of the embassy with whoever had accompanied him there, and that he should be virtually blackballed: no visas should be issued to anyone at his behest or on his La Cave Muzik sponsorship. Thus, so early on that morning, the visa exercise failed. All that was left was bleakness.

Onyeka took the next available flight to Paris. The pattern was familiar. After every unpleasant reversal, he would swiftly leave the scene, the city, and sometimes the country where the setback had occurred. He seemed determined to banish the upset from sight and memory.

Nevertheless, the failure that hurt him most stemmed from his inability to distinguish between musical acts, which merely wanted to use him, and those who genuinely sought success through him. In 2015 in Oguta, there was an incident that involved the Nigerian musician Etcetera (his real name is Ejikeme Paschal Ibe). Onyeka and I had been in Oguta over Christmas, working as part of the organizing team for the Njiko Cultural Festival. Etcetera called and texted continually, urging Onyeka's aid in actualizing his dreams, which were many. They included visiting the United States, promotion, managing, and advising. Onyeka, I understood, considered Etcetera a talented artist, and generally had more respect for artistes who could play at least one musical instrument, than for those unable to play any. Consequently, he took Etcetera, his artiste Dapo, and Oritsejolomi (whom he signed to his La Cave Musik label in 2014) to perform a closed jazz session at the American Consulate in Lagos. The Americans enjoyed themselves, and Onyeka later introduced Etcetera to them as his close associate. In the spirit of friendship and mutually understood goals, he instructed me to write an introduction letter for Etcetera, attesting that he was constitutive of our diplomatic jazz night initiative, and genuinely wished to participate in the AZULE writing and artistic residency in the U.S. Etcetera gratifyingly was given a 2-year U.S. Visa, and stopped answering Onyeka's calls and replying to his emails. Onyeka, who felt he had endured enough fickleness from Nigerian musicians, was crushed by this inconstancy. Etcetera had vowed that he would come to Abuja in February 2016 to perform at the Diplomatic Jazz Night at the Indian High Commission. That promise, it appeared, had been but a ruse for Onyeka to facilitate his acquisition of a U.S visa. Onyeka had actually intimated to me his goal of taking Etcetera to Europe for a music tour, country to country, city to city, but that plan of course could not materialize.

Visas, frankly, were the factor that bound many Nigerian artistes to Onyeka. Given that foreign missions in Nigeria seldom know them or their music, embassies treat them – as they do other Nigerians – with intense suspicion, expecting them to use their visiting Visas to get into European asylum establishments. Onyeka was the one who took these artistes by hand, introduced them to his friends who were Ambassadors or Consular officers, showed them the artistes' YouTube videos, and sometimes brought them to perform at embassy events, in order to establish that they were genuine musicians and not fronts. Indeed, the entire process of proving one's profession to the Euro-American Consulates reproduced and reinforced the power dynamics between the West and post-colonial Africa where Africans constantly have to justify why they should be trusted with a visa. At any rate, these interventions by Onyeka often broke the deadlock of instant and unwavering rejection for the artiste visa applicant. The artiste, Tekno, was once introduced to the Italian Consulate in Lagos by Onyeka, and was issued a month's visa. On seeing this, Onyeka took him back to the Consulate, showed the diplomats YouTube videos of the artiste which numbered in the millions. Impressed, they issued him a 6-month visa. Onyeka got Korede Bello his Canadian visa. Onyeka got Davido his first work visa to France to enable him to perform. I know these facts, and I can prove them. I wrote some of the letters supporting their applications.

Brymo was to an extent a casualty of Etcetera's ingratitude. Brymo's manager was hot on Onyeka's heels and wanted him to join their team. However, this was still at a time where we were both strenuously seeking sponsors of the impending Jazz Night. Onyeka not only loved but was practically beguiled by Brymo's music. Etcetera's conduct, however, made Onyeka feel that involvement in Nigerian musical acts was not worth the trouble.

One day, in conversation, when the contract controversy between Runtown and *Eric Many Entertainment* came up, an exasperated Onyeka told me: 'This is why I stopped signing artistes. This is what I don't understand about Nigerian musicians. The moment they get what they want, they turn against you. I'm not giving anybody one more contract. If you want partnership with me, it won't be on any written agreement, and so you can't say I owe you anything. They'll sit on their butt and wait for you to pay for their music production, to pay for their music videos, to get shows for them, to get visas for them, to promote their music. And soon as they think they've achieved something, they abandon you. They bite the hand that fed them.'

It was therefore no surprise that his relationship with many Nigerian artistes was fraught with controversies. This subject is treated in detail in his book, *Hip Hop is Only for Children*. So annoyed was Terry G by what Onyeka wrote about him that he plotted to have Onyeka beaten up. I also recall an occasion when Onyeka called Phyno, in my presence, and the rapper, rather annoyed, kept asking: 'Who gave you my number?' It was unbelievable that an artiste in this time and age would ask such a question rather than discuss the reason for the call. Onyeka, as a man genuinely keen on music and culture, is alert to manifestations of talent. He would rush to give opportunities to any unknown young talent whose creative output was promising or accomplished. This avidity for artistry made him acclaim Orliam, Dapo and later, John Bethel Ezeugo, whose song, *Ezeugo*, was written by Onyeka.

Orliam was already an established artiste, comfortable in his own world and in his own musical style. For Onyeka, if Asa was the Nigerian goddess of music, Orliam was the Nigerian god. He had actually toured with him in a number of European cities, and seen Orliam thrill crowds. That was why, at the maiden edition of the Diplomatic Jazz Night, Onyeka knelt before the Consul General in the visitors' lounge of the Italian Consulate in Lagos. He pleaded with the Consul General to forgive Orliam and allow him to play. Orliam had annoyed everyone at the Consulate with a stupid demand a few days earlier, causing the Consular to send Onyeka an angry message, directing that they no longer wanted to see Orliam's face at the Consulate. Later that night, Onyeka beamed with angelic smiles when Orlaim began to thrill everyone in the audience, including the hitherto grumpy Consular.

Dapo, whose real name is Oladapo Fasuyi, is a Jazz musician with a deep, sonorous voice. Onyeka fell in love with Dapo's music after listening to his song, *Insane*. In the beginning, their relationship was far from smooth.

While Dapo fancied himself as a finished product, Onyeka considered him still rough on the edges, still in need of polishing. Dapo felt a musician had 'arrived' if he could write and sing songs. To Onyeka, a musician's work required more than ability to sing. He believed a musician's persona, dressing, social media posts, hats, shoes, jackets, and other such factors determined the difference between a successful and a fumbling artiste. Many people could sing, but only a fraction of singers could sell music. Onyeka's insistence on shaping every aspect of Dapo's personality drew such resistance that Onyeka often simply let him be. On one occasion, when Dapo was scheduled to perform at a Jazz event, Onyeka gave him a special outfit to wear, and a hat as well, as those would interest his audience. 'And also, Dapo, please, I know you can sing, but raise your voice, shout, sit down on the stool there, hold the mic stand with one hand, and bend the mic to your lips with the other hand. You can tell your audience a story after each song, maybe the story that inspired the song. Tease them, ask them to sing along with you in some parts, keep them engaged, and that's how you carry the audience and lock them to yourself.'

Then Onyeka made a suggestion which might have irritated Dapo. 'Dapo, look at Orliam, look how he does it.' Dapo ignored every suggestion from Onyeka, went on stage, and did things his way. As Onyeka and I stood at a corner watching the performance, he held his chin in his hand, scratching his beard in apparent unease.

'I'm not sure Dapo wants to do music. He should find something else to do. He's kidding himself. How am I going to take him on tour to Europe like this?'

Despite everything, Dapo still saw Onyeka as the only person capable of making him a star, and Onyeka, in spite of his remarks at the show, was still interested in Dapo's career. It was not long after that that he took Dapo to South Africa to shoot the video of his song, *Beautiful*, which was dedicated to Asa. Shortly afterwards, Onyeka got him a visa to Italy to record his debut album, *In The Time of Suffering*.

This renewed working relationship would have its crescendo at the 2016 AMAA awards, when Onyeka ensured that Dapo was officially billed to perform on the stage of Africa's biggest movie awards ceremony. That night, less than a year after the lacklustre performance at that Jazz event, Onyeka and I again stood together, grinning as we listened to a transformed and captivating musician. Dapo had perfect control of the band, and reigned over the stage like a maestro.

He was loud, he was relaxed, he enjoyed himself, and the hall echoed the beauty of his sound. He was in charge. Onyeka was thrilled, and so was I, not only for Dapo but especially for Onyeka.

"This is an incredible performance," I told him. "What happened to Dapo?"

"I've been doing a lot of work with him. Lots of prepping. He started listening to me," he responded.

I would appear that the faith he reposed in Dapo had

begun to pay off. I remember Onyeka falling seriously ill on their way to South Africa. In South Africa, despite the infirmity, stress and jet lag, Onyeka managed to shoot the *Beautiful* music video. He then collapsed from exhaustion at the Oliver Tambo Airport in Johannesburg airport en-route to Nigeria. I'll never forget the picture of him being moved from the flight into the Lagos international airport on a wheelchair.

John Bethel's association with Onyeka began well, but suddenly the trajectory of both of his career and their relationship changed. He was barely 20 when he met Onyeka, who almost instantly took deep interest in him. John Bethel had a strong, crisp and loud voice that could ring across a loud auditorium without a microphone. He had taught himself the guitar and was fantastic at it. Further, he had dropped out of college (the University of Nigeria that Onyeka himself dropped out of), to pursue his musical dream. This shared experience may have specially endeared him to Onyeka!

Onyeka saw John Bethel's advancement as his personal project, and they got on well, not only due to John's drive and hunger, but because he regarded Onyeka almost as a godlike figure. In a short time, the young man's career began to flourish. He got opportunities to perform at high-profile events (back to back), flew into cities, lodged in good hotels, and granted radio interviews about his work. Denrele may have been his manager for most of his career, but Onyeka was the one who opened doors and cleared paths for him. To be fair,

John Bethel's commitment both to music and to Onyeka is indisputable, and on more than one occasion he gave Onyeka cause for pride and joy. At the Diplomatic Jazz Night at the Italian Consulate, he opened his performance with two Italian songs, rendered in a brisk, powerful and enchanting manner. Everyone stopped their conversation to gaze at him. Onyeka gave him a Spanish hat and a poncho and asked him to go barefoot on stage to perform. He did as he was advised, and at the show's end, every diplomat who was present not only congratulated him, but sought to know him personally.

Afterwards, Onyeka asked an elated John Bethel, 'Did I not tell you they would get interested if you packaged yourself like that?'

A week later, Onyeka was invited by the TEDx Jabi team to give a TED talk at the Ladi Kwali Hall in Sheraton Hotel, Abuja. Onyeka appeared undecided as to what to do with John Bethel, believing that in some situations, people had to be allowed to choose their future paths. In his hotel room, he presented John Bethel with 40,000 naira and told him: 'I'm giving you this for all your efforts and work you've put in; for yourself and alongside me. Do you want to take it and go home, or do you want me to use it to buy you a return ticket to Abuja, so you can perform at the TED event?'

His head bowed, John Bethel looked at the money, gazed at the tiled floor for all of 60 seconds, then raised his head and said, 'I want to play at the TED event.'

Onyeka was pleased, and would later tell me, "*Okwa*

71

ihuru nwa ma ihe? (Can you see his head is in the right place/ You see he is sensible?) A lot of young people would have taken the money and gone back to their parents' house and become useless again."

At the TEDx event, Onyeka showed up on stage with John Bethel who, once again, thrilled the TED crowd with novel and thrilling remixes of popular songs and his solo acoustic numbers. At the Njiko festival curated by Charles Oputa (Charley Boy) in Oguta, Imo State, Onyeka ensured that his artiste performed for a crowd of close to 1,500 people. The song, Ezeugo, which he rendered twice in two days, was on the lips of nearly everyone in Oguta. People recognized and hailed John Bethel everywhere we went. Onyeka finally shot the music video of the song in Oguta.

It is interesting that while Onyeka believes that neither Dapo nor John Bethel would be where they are today had it not been for him, both on the other hand feel that Onyeka failed to fulfill half of his lofty promises to them. They probably have a case. They could not have been the first persons to be promised much by Onyeka. I, too, was assured of a great deal, and numerous persons could say the same. Onyeka, for instance, said he would get me a book agent, pay for us to tour the world: that we would be in Paris together to organise the *Nollywood Week*, go to Abeokuta to interview the former President Obasanjo, and a few other assurances of delightful projects. Having been close to him, however, and been part of his daily existence, I knew that some of these objectives simply could not be realized, because he wrestled with his own demons and ambitions daily.

Some promises are made on the spur of the moment, in excitement; and some with firm resolve for their fulfillment. However, dreams can dream dreams of their own, peoples' plans fall apart, and they find themselves unable to keep their word. Renowned poet, Dike Chukwumerije, once said, 'Life is what happens when you are busy planning about life.' Being close to Onyeka enabled me to understand the man before he explained his actions to me. One who has not had such proximity to him might spend a lifetime resenting him for pledges he failed to honour. Indeed, he often felt he had made good his promises, but those mistaken beliefs only reflected his bipolar urges. After suffering the shock of his life when he visited Senator Anyanwu, who had promised him a million naira at the launch of his debut novel, he often told anyone who cared to listen: 'Not all promises are meant to be fulfilled.' Those were the exact words that the Senator spat at the face of a longsuffering 21-year-old boy who had paid him many anxious visits. Onyeka came to a lacerating realization. He had merely been fooled to expect one million naira, and all his visits to claim it had been a fool's errands. To this day, Onyeka could be unperturbed about breaking a promise, and readily quote the Senator's dismissive words: 'Not all promises are meant to be fulfilled.'

6

CONSOLATO D'ITALIA

The Story of the Diplomatic Jazz Night

We were at No. 12 Walter Carrington Crescent, Victoria Island. Onyeka and I were standing on the top floor of the Italian Consulate, hands folded and staring at the Atlantic Ocean before us. Neither of us spoke. We merely watched the water gently rock Otedola's yacht on the bay. Otedola's Forte Oil office was the building next to us. We had ridden out waves of turbulence to finally host the inaugural edition of the Diplomatic Jazz Night, a unique music-cultural initiative. This was happening on the 31st of October, 2015, some three months after Onyeka informed Andrea Pompamaier, Consul General of Italy in Lagos, of his wish to embark on the initiative. A month and four days before then, I had had a crucial meeting with Andrea and his personal assistant, Ella Obiako, to devise the operational framework of the event. It was also a month and three weeks after Onyeka woke up in Lima, Peru, with a paralysis that seemed so total that he could not move any part of his body, and doubted that he would ever walk again. It was also a month and two weeks since all who had promised us financial support reneged on their pledges. The Jazz Night was finally happening, the day after it appeared all our striving would end in futility. The Diplomatic Jazz Night happened! It began in rapturous vein, with one of the most adulatory introductions of Onyeka's career.

A delighted Andrea took the microphone. The hall, so hushed that the next person's heartbeat could be heard, awaited his opening remarks.

"I am happy to welcome everyone to this occasion. My name is Andrea Pompamaier. I am only the Consular General of Italy. But I want to present to you today, a man much more complicated than I am. He is a filmmaker, a writer, a music promoter, a cultural entrepreneur and businessman: Onyeka Nwelue. He's the one that put this whole thing together, and he may have some things to say to us."

Onyeka had envisaged the Jazz Night as an opportunity to promote music, language, creative expressions and a choice space for young Nigerian artists to reach varied audiences. He had deplored the dearth of fora for such artistic ventures. After our discussions with the Consul General's office, Mr. Pompamaier gave

Onyeka's dream not only legs to stand on but also wings to soar!

The intricacies of funding, hall and stage arrangements, sponsorship and audience were yet to be finalized. Consequently, when Onyeka informed the Consul General that we needed to host the maiden edition in a month's time, the diplomat sought an urgent meeting with him. Onyeka at the time was receiving treatment in an Indian hospital, and only managed to send emails from his hospital bed.

'You're the only one I trust right now to go and represent me at that meeting,' Onyeka's email to me read. 'We've been on this since day one. You know everything about the plan for this thing. The sponsors, the money issues, the artistes to perform, and so forth. I've just copied you in an email I sent him. You'll be contacted soon about the date the meeting will be taking place.'

I read the message, and took a deep breath. Several obstacles came to mind. I estimated the cost of flying to Lagos from Owerri, the cost of transportation within the city, the fact that I would need to stay at a hotel in Lekki or Ajah afterwards, and must return the following day to the office that paid my wages. I considered all the challenges and hitches the trip might cause, and drew a long deep breath, bracing myself for the undertaking. Knowing the fragility of Onyeka's health and finances at the time, I dispelled the urge to discuss the journey's monetary requirements with him.

'I was emailed today by the Consular's secretary, Joumana', I told him, 'and was asked to choose between two dates which was convenient. Friday, which is tomorrow, or Wednesday next week.'

'Go tomorrow,' Onyeka promptly urged, evincing his habitual aversion from procrastination. 'You may die before next week.' Briskness typified Onyeka. He continued: 'Something may happen, I may no longer be alive, the person you're going to see might fall ill, the Atlantic might decide to empty itself in the streets of Lagos, someone might send them a slanderous report about you, anything can happen... *Nnam*, go tomorrow and let's know our fate.'

The next day, my flight, which was delayed by 2 hours, arrived in Lagos at 3:20 pm, only 40 minutes before the scheduled time of the meeting. I asked the driver to 'do a Hamilton' if he could and *formula one* me to the Consulate so that I would not ruin my very first meeting with my revered host. This Nigerian airline, with habitual inability to adhere to its own flight schedules, had thrown the first spanner in the day's plans, but now that I was already in Lagos, I was determined to make it just in time. The young driver was beyond impressive, for when we reached Dodan Barracks, which was only a kilometre away from the Consulate destination, I had 15 minutes to spare. In Lagos, however, the traffic situation undergoes swift transformation. One should never assume they are punctual until one has actually arrived at a destination. With that negligible kilometre between me and the Consulate, a gridlock from hell itself interrupted the flow of traffic, so that I could only manage to arrive at the Consulate at 4.20 pm!

Mr. Pompamaier stepped into the reception lounge, visibly tired from the day's work, but welcomed me graciously with a hearty smile. A tall, amiable man. His hair was a mixture of blonde and grey. I began to apologize for my lateness, but he was swift to dispel my remorse, declaring himself happy that I could come at a day's notice. Ella, his Personal Assistant (PA), was beside him. Although elegant, she bore an officious demeanour that was somewhat unsettling. She listened to him, and iterated some of the Consul General's statements, which he did not think he might have expressed adequately, due to his limited command of English.

'Ehhh… You are looking at something like an event people will pay for entry, like set tables for VIPs, entry tickets?'

'It's the original plan, yes,' I answered, my voice indicating readiness to defer to his own ideas.

'You see, we're happy to support this project. Of course, this idea, I find it interesting. But you know, as a foreign mission, our premises cannot be used for certain transactional or commercial purposes. Both from a security and protocol perspective, it cannot be allowed. You know, standard procedure, basic rules every Consulate operates with.'

I listened to him, and I nodded gently and repeatedly. Although somewhat dismayed, I listened calmly until he was done. I had come with a paper containing a list of tentative partners we had contacted, and also intended to detail our funding plans. Those opening remarks were an early and unexpected blow. The document which bore my own negotiating projections had become painfully irrelevant.

Fucking hell! I thought. *How in the world are we supposed to fund this event if we aren't going to sell tickets?* At the same time, I acceded to the operational parameters Mr. Pompamaier continued to expound. I raised no arguments at all. Whatever issues were fuzzy, whatever grey areas remained, I would leave for Onyeka to address. He after all had a knack for finding solutions, and he had not sent me to make demands. What the Consulate offered – a fantastic venue, decorations, food and wine for all guests – were ample.

I asked if we could add a red carpet segment to the event, as we already had an agreement in principle with the African Movie Channel (AMC) to cover the event.

'No. We wouldn't want something like that' was the answer.

So, automatically, the media partners we had brought on board had become irrelevant. We no longer needed Wazobia FM to run radio jingles for the event. We did not need Linda Ikeji Blog to provide either pre-event or post-event publicity. We were not going to sell tickets, and to top off our woes, we faced the daunting task of finding the funds to stage an elaborate Jazz show.

When I was shown around the premises by the Consul General, I saw the mini amphitheatre, a lush-green outdoor lawn, and a beautiful and spacious lounge. The genial diplomat then turned to me and said, 'You're free to choose whichever location here you prefer to do the event.'

'The lounge is perfect,' I said without a second thought. He smiled, as though he knew I could not have chosen anywhere else but the lounge. 'How many people are you expecting to be present for the event?'

I try to process an answer as fast as I can. Onyeka and I had not made projections about expected numbers. Now that I had seen the venue, I could roughly assess the number that gracious salon could comfortably contain. 'We're expecting to have 25 people.'

'You mean, with the performers, and camera and journalist guys?' he asked.

'Yes, I think 50 in total would be a good fit for a place like this," I answered. "Twenty-five people from us, and maybe 25 or 30 people from you.'

'OK. I think that is fine. Of course, my colleagues in other Consulates will be here, and our own staff; yes, say altogether, 50. Fine. So, can you send me another proposal tonight?'

'Yes, sure. I'll just have to speak with Onyeka, and we'll come up with something that works for the Consulate and us' was my reply. He approved my suggestion, asking me to send him the document and also copy Ella. I thanked him.

It was 5:45 pm. I was delighted as I left the Consulate.

'You see why I said you should come and work alongside me,' an elated Onyeka wrote to me after reading my report of the meeting with the Consul General. 'What do you see in an obscure federal university in Abia State, *Nna m*?'

'That obscure university, that's what enabled me to pay for my flight and hotel bills to make this trip, you know?' I replied.

'I don't need to read it,' he said about the new proposal I had drawn up. 'I'm tired, and just recuperating at my sister's house now. I can't believe you've written a new proposal already. That's why I love you. Just send it to them and let's see what they say.'

The next few days were challenging. We made revisions to the document. Lots of adjustments were necessary: over the Consulate's preferred time for the event's commencement, on which day of the week it should hold, how to send out the invitations and who would do it. We also had to provide the names and occupations of our invitees. We adhered to all instructions, not because we could not afford not to – although we were not spoilt for choice, either – but because those at the Consulate were as enthusiastic about the programme as we were. We were told that the doors of the Consulate were open to us whenever we cared to come for sound-checks or other preparations.

'Where are you? *Nna m*, are you now in Lagos?' That was the first SMS I received as the plane touched the ground. My plan was to take a taxi to a hotel in Lekki, and in the morning join Onyeka at the agreed venue on Victoria Island. It had been one hell of a day. I had stood on my feet to deliver a two-and-a-half-hour lecture at the university, in a packed auditorium of about 700 students. After leaving the hall, drooping and sweating, I drove for an hour to Owerri airport, where I spent another hour seating out a flight delay, and finally landed in a Lagos teeming with chaos and traffic menace.

'Come to Ogudu,' Onyeka urged me. 'I've got a room for you already, Nna. *Biko*, bring your intelligent self here. I really need you around.'

Nothing I said would have convinced Onyeka that I had had a blinder of a day, and the only thing I needed was to be under a duvet sheet in an air-conditioned room. However, I accepted the burden of knowing Onyeka, or the price of being found valuable by Onyeka. To associate closely with him proved that you were of worth to him, which raised the presumption that you would share his work ethic. It meant being decisive, forsaking sleep, pursuing perfection, and above all, never yielding to fatigue.

At the hotel, I went to his room after dropping my bag in mine. There were many people, a situation that I had grown to expect. There could be no Onyeka without a crowd. We exchanged pleasantries and jokes.

'Short man, I know you've missed me,' he said to the hearing of everyone, and laughed.

'I missed you so much, I wanted to go to Lekki instead,' I retorted.

'*Shurrup* there *jor*, you like me too much, just like this one there with his big *nyash*,' he said, pointing at the Nigerian music producer, Bobby Combs. The room now erupted in boisterous laughter.

'I don't know what I've done to this boy,' Bobby said, 'Why can't this guy stop talking about my arse?' The laughter crescendoed.

'Can you walk comfortably on your feet now?' I asked Onyeka. He had been wheeled into Lagos International Airport about a month earlier. I knew he was using a walking aid, his spine was not fully set, his back still ached, and his steps were labored.

'I've dropped the walking aid. This is the most important event I'm organizing in my life; I won't go there on crutches. I stopped using it for a week now. I feel a bit of pain, but nothing will happen to me.'

At ten minutes to midnight, Onyeka told me we had to go to Surulere, a bustling district on the Lagos mainland.

'Surulere? But you know…' I began.

'Mitterand,' he called me by my real name this time. 'There is no sleep, Nna *m. Biko*. You have to follow me to supervise the rehearsal. I want your thoughts; I want you to have a look at what they're doing. My driver is already downstairs waiting for us.'

In Surulere, I was the first to get into the rehearsal studio. I exchanged greetings with Dapo, and then John Bethel. Orliam was absent.

'But where is Orliam? He's the star of the show, isn't he?' I asked Onyeka.

'Orliam fucked up,' he replied. 'Orliam nearly made the Consulate cancel the entire event. And now, he and his manager are ringing my phone non-stop.'

It happened that five days earlier, when Onyeka took the entire crew – artistes, cameramen, band players, stage decorators – for a sound check at the Consulate, something interesting occurred. Orliam was not convinced that we were having the show at no cost to the Consulate. He was resolute in his scepticism and suspected us of deviousness. He probably also thought that 'white' people always had money to throw around. Onyeka's assurances that he would not make money from the venture, but was rather spending money, did not convince Orliam. As a professional musician who must have worked with a number of show organisers and promoters, it is possible that Orliam might have faced situations in which these event organisers cheated him out of deals. So his scepticism was not irrational.

Orliam went behind Onyeka's back to the Consulate and asked to see Mr. Pompamaier. One could only imagine the diplomat's shock when Orliam presented him with an invoice. He was requesting to be paid a certain amount of money by the Consulate for his performance. A seasoned diplomat, Andrea took the invoice without asking any questions and simply told him the Consulate would contact him.

After a few failed attempts at reaching Onyeka by phone, the Consulate, livid at what they considered an insulting visit, sent Onyeka an email which simply read: 'You've broken all our agreements, Onyeka.' Was Onyeka fooling them? Did Onyeka not tell the artistes that the Consulate was bearing no costs for their performances? Was Onyeka expecting them to assume artistes' welfare contrary to the initial agreement? Was Onyeka a greedy, sneaky, slippery Nigerian intent on deception? The Consulate was so irked that it called and sought explanations from the two other performing artistes.

On the phone with Dapo, a diplomat asked, 'What is your agreement with Onyeka about getting paid for the show?' Dapo replied, 'Onyeka told me I'm performing for free. We didn't discuss anything about money.'

John Bethel was called, and gave the same answer. The Consulate them surmised that Orliam had acted on his own behind Onyeka's back. This was five days before the event. Although Onyeka had planned to return to Lagos three days before the event, he boarded a flight to Lagos immediately he saw the Consulate's email, and hastened to the Consulate to salvage the performance and clear his name.

Before Onyeka arrived in Lagos, however, the Consulate called Orliam to tell him he would no longer be performing. 'Your part of the show is cancelled' was the categorical bar. Although Orliam was, unquestionably a fantastic artiste, his action was interpreted as opportunistic and self-serving. It had of course outraged the Consulate. When Onyeka arrived to tender profuse apologies, the Consulate accepted his regrets, agreed that the event would proceed as planned, but was inflexible over the proviso that Orliam must not feature.

Onyeka, however, now faced a new dilemma. The tower banner for the event bore Orliam's face, and so did the event leaflet for guests. It would be unthinkable not to have the banner at the event. It would also appear demented not to feature the proclaimed star of the show, when the leaflet detailed his life and attainments. Interestingly, even after Onyeka had begun to envisage the show without Orliam, he still hoped that the situation might somehow be changed. Without Orliam, it could not be the show he had hoped for.

After two hours at the rehearsal, Onyeka, dissatisfied with what he had seen, rose to address the band. 'Guys, look, I've attended hundreds of live events, in Europe and across Africa. I can tell you now that you're a very talented band. But live performances, like the one we're going for tomorrow, need heart. Need passion. All live performances need uncommon energy. You need to show that you're happy doing what you're doing, because that's the only way the best of you will come out. And that is how you'll mesmerize your audience. This is not just a band for tomorrow. I am not hiring you guys for a one-off event. I have seen greatness in this band, and I'm already making plans to tour with you guys in Europe later on. Tomorrow is a big day; we should bring our best.'

After that pep talk, the next one hour of rehearsal was amazing. We both felt that the concert had begun. I grinned at Onyeka, whose cheeky reaction was 'why are you smiling? Short Professor! Let's go home. It's 3 AM.'

I never explained why the smile was on my face. I did not need to. He understood. I just witnessed the most effective choreographed lie of my life. Onyeka was never going to take the boys to Europe, certainly not at any time in the near future as he had indicated. He knew that Nigerians could lay down their lives for someone who made them grandiose promises. That, after all, explained the mindset of people who gave half their salaries to their pastors, because they were promised Dangote[7] riches, for 'sowing a seed.' I saw Onyeka delve into the souls of those boys to extract the best they could give, before moving on. He could sometimes shut down the moral arteries that precluded people from using

---

7   Aliko Dangote was considered the wealthiest man in Africa.

others. However, he also understood that only material gain – or the expectation of it – could inspire most people to perfectionist diligence. He had resolved that if lying to people to make them give their best made him seem like the devil, so be it. Someone would probably just as remorselessly use and dump him the following day. In Nigeria, this cycle was organically self-reinforcing. People who are used, use others and await their karma! That rehearsal was one of the occasions when I wondered if I could ever become so adept at lying, so capable of making people yield their souls for a promise I never intended to keep. I duly answered my own question. *No, I can't. Onyeka needs me for things I am comfortable at doing, while he handles other tasks that I'd hate to discharge.*

By 2 pm on the day of the event, we were on our way to the Consulate. Although it was scheduled to start at 6 pm, there were many preliminary matters to attend to. We had to make sure the sound, lights and reverberations were right. Onyeka also needed time to work his magic. He had not given up on Orliam performing at the show, despite my saying it would take a miracle for that to happen.

Before we left for the Consulate, he had gazed at the roll-banner in the hotel room. A beautiful piece of work, it read: 'Blues & Hills Consultancy in Collaboration with the Consulate of Italy, Lagos invites you…' He beamed a weary smile, and stared at the banner for over ten minutes, swallowing, sighing, stroking his chin, intermittently removing his hat and putting it back on. Shortly after, as though assailed by apprehension, he paced around the room in obvious unease. When he sat on the sofa, he reclined to relax, but shortly sat up on the sofa's edge. 'There has to be a way,' Onyeka finally said, and I knew it was about the Orliam situation.

We got into a conversation that went round and round in circles, over whether or not to take the banner to the Consulate. If Orliam was not going to perform, why take the banner? If he should appear by some last-minute reversal, why leave the banner behind? Onyeka finally said: 'We take it, right? What do you think? We take it. We take it. Yeah, we take it. We'll be putting it in a rack anyway, so we don't have to pull it out if the Consul General doesn't listen to this last plea.'

In the car, he informed me that the Consulate did not send invitations to all the celebrities he wished to invite, like Genevieve Nnaji, Linda Ikeji and Tony Elumelu. He could not tell for what reason exactly, and concluded: 'They have their way. They'd have their reasons.'

At the Consulate, Onyeka met with Ella the PA. Mr. Pompamaier, seeing us, strode past us in a chilly snub! The tables were set; wines were already set on the tables for those who wanted a drink before the show. Ella and I exchanged greetings: cold, officious hellos. Ella is a nice person, but there was a bossy side to her that was all too apparent. She paid great attention to detail. Any boss would be glad to have a personal assistant like her – she evinced no laxity. In mine and Onyeka's views, Ella was the most dedicated and capable staff anyone could have. However, I retained the feeling that she was not overly fond of me. I sensed this, because I can be a little too self-assured, a trait that is easily mistaken for arrogance. Onyeka went down on his knees to plead Orliam's case. Somehow, I never felt all the grovelling was necessary. Onyeka, however, sought what he sought, and would go to great lengths to gain it. I moved to the window that overlooked the stage, and fiddled with my phone.

'You didn't need to do all that groveling though,' I finally told him, when I saw he had emerged from his meeting with Ella.

'Pray that one day you do not need people, Mitt,' he replied. 'Me, I am shameless. I even told her I was willing to lie down, not just kneel, just so she sees how sorry I am.'

Minutes later, the Consul General walked in. 'Is it my fault, Onyeka?' he asked. 'Is it my fault that you broke our agreements?'

'No, sir,' Onyeka pleaded. 'No. I take full responsibility. I am sorry. I am very sorry for what he did.'

'He can come and play. Orliam. He is free to come and play, but just for today,' the Consul General pronounced.

Onyeka looked at me. It was incredible. Ella had performed her magic, and to this day, Onyeka calls her 'Your Majesty'. Their affection and esteem remain unwavering. We immediately unfurled the banner. Orliam joined us in less than 30 minutes, which could only have meant that he and his crew had been ready and nearby, hopeful that Onyeka would once more pull a rabbit out of a hat. Of course he did!

That evening, as Orliam stepped up to the stage, he asked for the lights in the room to be turned off, leaving only two mini bulbs, beaming directly at his head, leaving his band members wreathed in blue and yellow illumination. The entire room was then stilled. With that, Orliam had given us a hint of the delights he bore, and we waited impatiently for more.

Soon, his deep, sonorous voice was striking and bouncing off the walls, his bearded face reflecting a soul that was a happy custodian of soulful melodies. Orliam sang in languages we understood, and those we only pretended to understand. We were blissfully borne along by the current of his genius. Gradually, Andrea, the other Consulates, Onyeka, myself, the security men in plain clothes, the waiters and everyone else it seemed, moved from where they stood to the front of the stage. We were all captivated, and would not have hesitated to jump into Orliam's mouth. This was a jazz band that seemed more like an orchestra. I now understood why Onyeka had so exerted himself to get Orliam to play there. Months later, in conversation, Orliam told me that he sometimes heard voices ordering him to his piano.

'I hear these voices. They tell me, no they command me: "Go! Go, Orliam! It's time to get that music on. It's time to sing." And they are happy. I communicate with these spirits. Those things I say...'

"You mean the *ding dan dere, dara dara?*" I asked.

He smiled, and said, 'They understand me. I think everyone understands when I speak that language during my performances too.'

It was not much of a surprise. Orliam rehearses and sings with a skill and ease that can only exist in a man whose music transcends the physical realm.

The show ended with Orliam's sublime performance. More wine, lasagne, pizza margherita, risotto, and cakes were dispensed, and no one seemed anxious to leave. The High Commissioner of Canada, asked Onyeka, 'What would it cost to organize something like this at the Canadian High Commission?' Onyeka replied. 'Nothing, Your Excellency.'

'Nothing?' repeated the diplomat. 'Could we do it next weekend, then?'

Before we left, Onyeka introduced me to Aboyeji Iyinoluwa.

'This is Professor Mitterand,' he said. It was how he always introduced me. I would then, abashed and uneasy, tell the new contact: 'I'm no Professor; he's just kidding.' Aboyeji, who co-founded a start-up named Andela (and years later Flutterwave), would nine months later win a 24-million-dollar funding round from the Mark Zuckerberg Foundation. He duly brought the founder of Facebook to Nigeria in that luminary's first visit to Sub-Saharan Africa.

We began to leave, and met the Consul General on our way out. He appeared pleasantly surprised by the evening's triumph, and admitted it to Onyeka. I imagine that among his peers in the lounge, that diplomat felt a few inches taller. He obviously wished to say more, but was unable to find the words to express his delight. He sighed, blinked, and told Onyeka, 'Here is your home now.'

Onyeka looked at him and smiled. He too appeared short of words. We all were, until we got into our cab. It had taken a great deal to get to that stage. Money, time, energy, and steely tenacity had been deployed. The Jazz Night had come and gone, and was successful beyond Onyeka's wildest expectations. We left, penniless but ecstatic.

Orliam's song, *Life is Beautiful,* from his album, *Now Classic,* was playing in the car. We all demanded, almost simultaneously, that the driver should raise its volume. The driver raced across the Lagos Third Mainland

Bridge, his tyres thudding as we sped past each of the bridge's dividers. We waited for the song's chorus to chime in: *"...and we go higher higher higher – we go oh oh! We got confidence, we got confidence, and we got confidence now..."*

The lyrics reflected the elations and excitement in our spirits.

A week later, Italy's biggest English newspaper, *Italian Insider*, carried the story of the inaugural Diplomatic Jazz Night.

7

AFRICAN MOVIE ACADEMY AWARDS 2016

On June 11, 2016, I was travelling from Umuahia to Port Harcourt on the ludicrously horrible Enugu – Port Harcourt expressway. So damaged was this road that someone journeying in a roofless car, who neglected to use a seatbelt, could easily be jerked from their car into a pothole. The pains of the trip were compounded by the numerous security stops on the road. They impelled the feeling that Nigeria's Southeast had become a garrison. A police checkpoint here, an army check there, the Civil Defence Corps and Road Safety agents swooping down on motorists. I reached Port Harcourt in decent time, and had a few hours for a nap before getting ready for the night's event. Africa's excellence in motion pictures was being celebrated by the Africa Movie Academy Awards (AMAA) and I was tingling in anticipation.

At 7 pm, I was at the venue, the Obi Wali Cultural Centre. As I had neither a ticket nor a pass, I could not enter the hall. I found a comfortable corner on the terrace of the centre, and watched the arriving celebrities and dignitaries. There were exquisite young ladies in some of the most elegant and spectacular outfits I had ever seen. Some of the gowns – with trains or extended skirts – had to be held by the wearers' followers or fans to avoid the fabrics' irredeemable soiling or trampling. It was interesting to view the seeming conviviality of the couples who marched up. Some of the men held their wives with a pious tenderness which suggested that they could never contemplate a liaison with other women! From where I stood, I also saw the Information Minister, Lai Mohammed, arrive. Attended by Secret Service men, wearing his habitual long brown caftan with a white neckline, he was ushered through the VIP entrance.

Excitement and tension infused the atmosphere when Nyesom Wike, the Governor of Rivers State and special guest of honour, arrived. He did so in a majestic Mercedes APG, an armoured vehicle the size of a 2-bedroom bungalow, flanked on both sides by four armoured Land Cruisers. As the jungle safety protocol of Nigeria demanded, no other car was to be allowed into the premises until he left. I recall the frenzied – indeed theatrical – security clearing that preceded the Governor's emergence from his car. Aides, each trying to surpass the other, ruthlessly shoved people away. They seemed to feel they must sanitise the environment from vermin and barbarians. By the time the red carpet was eventually rolled out to herald the Governor's arrival, he was surrounded by a sea of black-suited DSS men so that no part of him was visible to anyone. It was obvious that some personage was strolling into the hall, but the dignitary could not be seen. The spectacle was nauseating. However, moments later, backstage, I encountered Wike's geniality. He was unassuming, and readily obliged those who wanted a photograph with him. I later pondered the difference between the natural disposition of some 'big men,' and the aggressive choreography of power enacted around them by aides or lackeys.

Onyeka, whom I had been waiting for, finally arrived at the entrance. I saw him before he had to search for me. 'You still smell of Paris, *Nna m*,' I teased.

'Hehe! Madman. Take this!' He handed me a Full Access Pass, which guaranteed me entry into all enclaves of that hall, including the exclusive backstage where the juiciest dramas unfold. We sauntered onto the red carpet corner. Progress was laboured as the space teemed with tower video cameras, light mechanism, media personalities seeking interviews and guests wanting to take photographs by the sponsorship wall. Shibi, the Zimbabwean photographer barged into us.

'This is Onyeka,' he said with a warm smile. 'I read everything you write on Facebook. I'm in love with your mind.'

A delighted Onyeka erupted in gales of laughter. They obviously knew each other. 'I would have loved for us to meet again. I'm on my way to South Africa tomorrow,' Shibi disclosed, and Onyeka replied: 'Actually, Sir, I'll be in South Africa for the Durban Film Festival.'

'That is lovely, I'm definitely looking forward to seeing you there,' declared Shibi.

Lorenzo Menakaya, a Nollywood actor and one of the organisers of the AMAA, walked up to us, clad in *babariga* and a red Igbo chief's cap. He complimented Onyeka: "*Nna*, you're looking so fine tonight. How come? Where did you borrow this cloth you're wearing?" Everyone, including Lorenzo the teaser himself, burst into laughter.

'*Enyi gi nwanyi kwa nu?*' I asked Onyeka as we moved into the event hall. He replied: 'She's somewhere in the crowd, sitting.' I was surprised that Onyeka did not have his girlfriend beside him, but then, this was Onyeka. Her presence would have been inhibiting for him. I discerned that he was not keen on discussing her, as he had done a few days earlier. They had flown into Nigeria together from Paris, and it was one of the reasons he said I must come to AMAA.

'Everybody will be there,' he had enthused. 'David Nnaji, my girlfriend, Aunty Peace... I need you to come, *Nna*.' Somehow, it reminded me of his plea to follow him to his hometown, Ezeoke. It truly appeared that there were things he longed for me to see, but did not want to tell me about beforehand. I had grown to know the man so well that I could tell from his intonation when he desperately wanted something. I, who was supposed to be flying to Rome that Saturday, gave him my word.

When I reached the AMAA backstage with Onyeka, I encountered flurries and flamboyance. There were a few empty seats, security bouncers built like tanks, a large event-monitor with Peace Anyiam-Osigwe sitting in front of it. The Director of the Programme, Segun Arinze, stood beside her. Mike Ezuruonye was the Master of Ceremonies. Segun appeared an absolute genius in his navigation of tasks, and Mike Ezuruonye was just as adroit. I felt he had a certain attribute that he tried to mask. I felt that, because I share the same trait. Actor, Uchemba Williams, whose chubby cheeks Onyeka joked about throughout the night, was keen on taking photographs with every celebrity backstage, gleeful and frisky as a child at the sight of chocolate candy.

I saw Onyeka approach Peace, and squat between her and Segun Arinze. They seemed to be sharing mother-and-son moments. I gazed long at Peace. She looked frail, and spoke very gently. However, she appeared totally focused on the large monitor in front of her, giving instructions from where she sat. It was easy to draw parallels between hers and Onyeka's lives. I began to realize Onyeka not only emulated Peace's stance on various issues, but wished to be Peace all through. I again looked at Peace, and beheld an enigma. She did not rise from her seat; the world went to her there. Everything was happening around her, but she was confident as the pivot from which all activity flowed. Only when David Mark (former President of the Nigerian Senate) and Governor Wike arrived backstage, did she rise, albeit with some discomfort.

Pete Edochie walked in, and for a moment it seemed that half the entire backstage instantly vanished. This was a colossus, both in career and physique. Segun Arinze hailed him in words that were indistinct but which were accompanied by a bow of the head, so one could tell that whatever Segun said was adulatory.

In his rich baritone that had graced numerous Nollywood movies, he enquired: *'Nna, ke kai mere?'* (How do you do?)

'Odi mma, Sir. Nnoo. Biko k'am wetelu gi oche.' Segun pulled up a seat for him. Their ensuing conversation was held entirely in Igbo.

When later the renowned Richard Mofe-Damijo (widely known as RMD) entered, the room was swiftly filled with reporters, and presumably with the screen-struck as well. RMD was being given the lifetime achievement award, along with Olu Jacobs and Pete Edochie. RMD, who was at the time a commissioner in his home state in Nigeria (Delta), gave one of the greatest acceptance speeches I had ever heard in my life. The entire hall erupted, all of the backstage rose to our feet, and even Peace herself smiled and clapped as he spoke. That was definitely the crescendo of the show, which only minutes earlier had struck a dreadful patch.

I recall that around 11:45 pm, Yinka Davies, (who in my opinion must make heaven if a beautiful voice were the qualification) had held the audience spellbound for all of five minutes. No sooner had she returned backstage than a total power outage plunged the entire building into darkness. My first thought was what a security row that hiatus would cause. A State Governor, a Minister of the Federal Republic, and a Senator who only the previous year had been the Senate President, all suddenly enveloped in darkness? It might be remarked that these high officials, although fawned upon in public, were not the best-liked people in Nigeria.

Complaints were heard that the generator had broken down again. 'It's a ploy. It's a bloody ploy to rip money off this woman,' Onyeka whispered, alluding to Peace. 'This same thing happened earlier today. After the generator was used for setting up the equipment and for rehearsals, when the event was about to start, they came to complain that it had broken down. You see why this country can never be better?'

As we murmured in the dark, Onyeka was quick to detect Peace's voice. It was a muted sob in the background. It was not too dim for him to find and embrace Peace. '*Emele nu ihe a nu, biko nu?*' (Don't do this, please?)

'Onyeka, they have sabotaged me,' Peace replied.

'*Ibekwanu akwa, ole kwanu ihe munwa g'eme?*' (If you cry, what do you want me to do?) Onyeka consoled, urging her to be stronger. Peace, surprisingly and gratifyingly, gave a hearty laugh. Their interaction had been brief and decisive, and I doubt if anyone else noted it. At the hotel the following morning, Onyeka recalled the issue, and told me how terrible he felt whenever Peace appeared hurt or vulnerable. 'Nigerians, industry people,' he maintained, 'do not deserve to see her tears; they should never be in a position to see her cry, especially because seeing her so vulnerable makes them delighted about their sorry lives.'

In my estimation, if Peace had a male doppelganger, it would be Onyeka. She was an exceptional organiser, of events as well as people. Considering the overwhelming challenges of producing an event like the AMAA, Peace could be described as superhuman. She had the clout to invite high political figures – and her invitations were honoured. I believe many industry colleagues were baffled by her power, and loathed her for it. She, however, earned the esteem of her contemporaries. She had a drive and grit that even bitter foes would respect. I could be describing Onyeka here, only that he seemed a less emotional person than Peace. He was cautious in dealing with people, always careful not to be at others' mercy. He seemed to have made a secret vow never to be in a situation beyond help or rescue.

Halfway through the show, Harry Songs came on stage, and everywhere was buzzing. 'Share the gala, share the booze, a booze, a booze,' he chanted and the hall erupted in a frenzy of bodies moving in random formations. His song, *Reggae Blues* was a nationwide sensation at the time. He was shortly joined by Kcee, his then label mate and the artiste featured on the song. Kcee hopped on stage immediately it was time for his own verse of the song. His performance was meant to end then, as he was not invited to perform a song of his own. HarrySong**s** left the stage as soon as the Reggae Blues performance ended. However, it appeared Kcee – and possibly his manager – had made their own plans. Performing the Reggae Blues song provided the perfect pretext for having Kcee on stage in the first place; and whilst there, Kcee slipped in a performance that was not in the programme. It seemed a little sinister, although laughable at the same time. Before anyone knew what was happening, we were watching through the backroom monitor, screaming, "Girl I want to see your face…"

Onyeka was outraged. "Onye *a onokwanu ebe ahu eme gini?* Why is he there? Who's paying him?" he asked to the hearing of Peace and Segun Arinze.

Peace was not having any of it either, and in fact seemed more infuriated than anyone else. 'What is that boy doing on my stage? Someone cut the sound!' Peace shouted from where she sat.

Both were clearly livid, but Onyeka especially so because Kcee was appropriating the slot reserved for

Onyeka's own artiste, Dapo. More annoying was the fact that Dapo had been there since morning, rehearsing with the five-man band. It could have been nothing but galling to find someone who was not billed, performing by sheer daring and stealth. Segun Arinze assured Peace that he could resolve the situation without abruptly cutting off sound. Taking that precipitate course would somehow have marred the entire evening. Kcee was eventually signalled to leave the stage, not only by Segun, but also by his manager. It mattered little to him at that stage. He had put in a 5-minute performance, and must have been elated by the crowd's acclaim.

Reflecting on the Kcee situation later on, I jokingly asked Onyeka if artistes had begun performing for free. 'Hehehehe! *I no dey house o!*' was his response. It appeared that the volcano of fury that erupted in his soul that evening had subsided completely. That was typical Onyeka. He had a very large heart, but never used it to harbour grudges or bitterness. I knew that he would have no objections to a professional collaboration with Kcee the following day, if the terms were promising. His disposition explained why he repulsed people's attempts to rope him into their personal feuds. He understood that the world proceeded in circles, and one never knew who might be helpful at any stage of life's journey.

'I may have enemies today, but they become friends tomorrow. I don't have any enemies.' That was one of the laws of in his rulebook. In fact, I was aware of how much he resisted gossip mongers who kept baiting him to reply to an article by his friend, Pearl Osibu, in which Pearl called Onyeka 'a Linda Ikeji arse-licker.' Onyeka never responded, but was shortly seen in Pearl's kitchen sharing a meal with her.

If AMAA had thrown up surprises, the morning after would dispense more revelations. I was woken up by insistent knocking on my door. When I asked who the caller was and got no reply, I knew it was Onyeka. I knew that whatever had awoken him that early had to be serious. If he had been in good spirits, he would have answered my question with one of his obscene jibes: 'Open the door, you cunt!'

His silence proved that we would have an enervating morning. 'Why are you here this early?' I queried. 'This is the hour of day when all penises rise with their owners. Shouldn't you be getting it on with your lady?'

'I haven't spoken to her since we got home last night,' Onyeka told me 'I don't know why these women think they can control a man's life.' He opened the fridge to fetch a bottle of Martini I had brought, then dialed the hotel reception for two glasses.

I knew my friend had his ways, and his ideas about love were peculiar. The girl in question, however, was someone he was convinced he felt special about. At various times, he had remarked that she was the only woman capable of understanding that he was not like anyone else, and that she consequently accommodated his eccentricities. When he discussed the girl, it was apparent that he was truly happy that there was a woman who understood his complexity and quirkiness.

On that morning, as he discussed the cracks that were appearing in their relationship, Onyeka sounded weary. He spoke in resigned tones, as though he had already accepted that their affair would end. 'My mum has lived with my father for thirty-five years. She never spoke to him for once the way this girl spoke to me last night. No one has ever spoken to me that way, not my siblings, not any of my friends, not even my parents.'

I had no idea he still hurt from her antics the previous night, when we had hung out together. I recalled the young lady saying, 'Onyeka, leave that stupid condom you're trying to buy and come pay for my chocolates!'

While Onyeka did not react then, his soul-baring that morning proved he was unable to push her words aside, and that his ego had been bruised. She had slighted him in the presence of all his male friends, mostly people who looked up to him.

In my understanding, his girlfriend's jibe probably sprang from pent-up frustration. She sulked for much of the AMAA night, because Onyeka was engrossed in organizational duties, and did not strut with her as a loving, glamorous couple. At the end of the AMAA event, we all trooped to a setting called Casablanca. Surrounded by open bars, it is also a noted prostitutes' hub in Port Harcourt. Onyeka exercised his loquacity, prattling almost flirtatiously with the prostitutes to draw cheers. This, predictably, offended his girlfriend. He had pleaded earlier to take her home so that he could hang out with his friends, as it was already 3 am. She insisted she would accompany him and his friends to wherever their destination was. It was not in Onyeka's nature to repress his effervescence for anyone, so her eventual moroseness was rather inevitable.

He turned to me, Martini glass in hand, and said, 'She never came across to me like that, you know? I never thought she'd be clingy like that. I'm tired, Mitt, I'm tired.'

Dapo joined us, and while sipping our drinks, we spoke of our impending rendezvous in Rome. Mere minutes into our camaraderie, there was another knock on the door. It could have been anybody, because AMAA had lodged a considerable number of people (some of whom were Onyeka's friends) in the same hotel.

Dapo asked who was knocking. I did as well, but there was no response. Then Onyeka repeated the enquiry we had made, and a mild voice from behind the door requested: 'Open, it's me.'

'It's you who?' Dapo and I roared almost simultaneously. The Martini was fast taking effect!

'Come in,' Onyeka eventually invited. 'The door is not locked.'

She pushed the door open, and stood outside. She was focused squarely on Onyeka, saying no hellos, indeed uttering no greetings, or acknowledging that there were two other people in the room beside her man. In the tones of an African mother summoning a petulant child, she told Onyeka, 'I need to see you now.' She repeated, 'Onyeka, come; let's go to the room. We need to talk now.'

'I'm coming later; I'm not done with what I'm doing here. Go. I'll come later' was Onyeka's response.

She didn't leave, but again issued a command. Onyeka again responded, 'I'll be there later.'

She backed away from the door, annoyed and showing it by not bothering to close the door she had opened. I recall unfreezing my breath at that moment, as the confrontation had tensed the room, and we were all craving a respite. Onyeka took another sip of his drink and began to discuss how he felt women carried much tension with them.

'I spoke to David Nnaji yesterday,' he told us, visibly keen on unburdening his soul. 'David is no longer with Jodie. It must have been a hell of a nightmare for the guy. He was crying. David, my friend! Never seen a grown man cry that much in a while. I can't even begin to explain here the hell he survived in that house. Look at all the drama my own girlfriend is putting up here. I never saw my mother order my father about like that, or speak to him in such a condescending way. These girls *gakwa gbara ogwu ha nuo o*.' (These women should mind themselves).

We knew he spoke in seriousness, even in distress, but it was hard not to laugh at the last sentence. He turned to me and declared: '*Nna, ike agwula m*.'

I felt sincerely sorry for him. Once a man said he was tired of a woman, with that facial expression, that wrinkled face, and half shut eyes, you knew he would not suffer the affair a moment longer.

By 11am that morning, my bags were packed and I readied myself to drive back to Umuahia, aware that I had a Monday morning class to teach. As Onyeka saw me off, walking down the corridor, he asked me to come to his room and be introduced to his lady, if only in adherence to etiquette. When he opened the door of his room, however, the room was vacant.

Onyeka looked around, exhaled, and said: 'She left. None of her things are here. She got angry and left.'

I reflected and said, 'Well, I don't know what to say. Just find a way to patch things up with her.' I did not believe the rupture was patchable, but I had to say something.

'Never seen someone so self-centred,' Onyeka reflected. 'You know, I can't even wear headphones if she's watching a movie, so she can laugh out loud and tell me when someone says something funny in the film. Who does that? No. No woman is going to control my life.'

Minutes later, I was speeding away from Port Harcourt, back to where I came from. This time, the road to home was scarier and bumpier than it had ever been. The potholes had become hellholes and death-holes. In some parts, the asphalt had not only cracked, but also been helped by rainfall to form craters. It was unbelievable that an oil-producing nation could have roads that were so bad. Surprisingly, I met one of the nicest army officers ever at the Oyigbo (Obigbo) Checkpoint. We shared a joke – two jokes, I think – and he waved me on. The officer had been so courteous and funny that I was tempted to park and have a longer chat with him. His disposition recalled the classic movie, *An Officer and a Gentleman*.

8

THE DOCUMENTARY

'It is hard not to fall in love with *The House of Nwapa*, Onyeka Nwelue's free-wheeling documentary on Flora Nwapa, the enigmatic writer who died in 1993. Reader, be warned, Onyeka Nwelue courts controversies and lives and breathes by them, and this documentary is no exception.'

That was how Pa Ikhide, Nigeria's most followed literary critic, opened his detailed review of Onyeka's *The House of Nwapa* documentary. Somewhere down the review, Ikhide, ever generous alike in compliments and criticism, delivered what seemed both a pat on the back and a *koboko* lash to the backside. Onyeka, he reckoned, 'comes across as a thinker and a doer, albeit a sloppy worker.' With this, even I would agree, and I dare add, even Onyeka would concur. Ikhide was right. When

Onyeka sets out to do things, his sights are focused more on the ultimate goal, and less on the fine points and aesthetics of the process.

This was the vein in which the documentary was made. Filmed over a period of 9 months, it started in August 2015 with the interview of Professor of Anthropology Sabine Jen Bahlsen in Berlin, and ended in May 2016. I was present when the first member of the Nwapa family – Flora Nwapa's younger sister Mrs Weruche Emeruem – was interviewed. It took place somewhere in St. Michael's Road Aba. Mrs. Emeruem gave an insider's account of Flora Nwapa's personality, her love life with her husband (and now widower) Gogo Nwakuche. She also insisted that her sister's death was not borne of natural causes.

There in Aba, I had seen Onyeka suffer severe back pain following treatment for lumbago. A few weeks earlier in Peru, he had woken up paralyzed in his bed. Onyeka had gone to Peru to participate in a literary festival, and also unveil the Spanish edition of his poetry collection *Quemando* (Burnt). In Chile, he had woken up one morning and been unable to rise from his bed. His eyes were open, but he found himself apparently stuck to the sheets. 'Thankfully,' he told me, 'I had developed the habit of having my laptop on my bed while I slept. All I did was use it to send a message to one of the event organizers. It was that lady who brought the ambulance that wheeled me from my room.' With this, I understood better the urgency with which he undertook the filming.

He became a time-wolf, preying on every dawn that broke.

'*Nna*,' I advised as I watched him struggle with his crutches, 'shouldn't you pay attention to your health first and return to this later?' I was worried that he might strain himself to the point of irredeemable damage. One needed to be alive, after all, to shoot a documentary.

'No. No, Mitt. What if I die tomorrow?' he said, his brows furrowed in a defiant frown. Nothing was going to deter him.

When the finished work was sent to his friend, award-winning filmmaker Tope Oshin, it returned with a barrage of corrections and criticism that made it seem the entire project should be overhauled.

Onyeka, however, soldiered on. Lots of cutting adjusting, colour grading, and other editorial efforts went into the film, so that it took another two months for the documentary to be finished. After undergoing that onerous process, Onyeka believed the world owed him a resonant applause.

He premiered it at the International Women's Film Festival in Harare. He had it screened at Ohio University. He had it shown at top-notch Harvard University. He often reacted to criticism like a Teflon Don, a creative to whom the pangs of scathing criticisms were utterly blunted. However, he was very much human, with a vulnerable soul, and offended by denunciations of his artistic productions. It was probably the best thing to do, in his position, to strive to be aloof from criticism, not only for his inner peace, but to deny real or imagined traducers the joy of seeing him downcast. I felt that a lot of people, under a facade of friendship with Onyeka, disliked his grit. Seen sometimes as extremely conceited, hated for his access to the powerful, many could not distinguish between the man and his works. Onyeka felt the film would be hated merely because it was his product! He expected some to disparage the product, not because it was defective, but because they disliked him. This was troubling, because, although he had shown it to Western audiences, it was the approbation of Nigerians that he desired most.

Oris Aigbokhaevbolo, one of Nigeria's most prominent film critics, and the very first to review the work, struck a raw nerve with his criticism, and characteristically 'took no prisoners.' Oris is no hater. I consider him a genuinely warm-hearted person. In fact, I would say he is actually good friends with Onyeka.

In his short review, however, Oris described the documentary as 'a rambling piece of cinema.' He added that he perceived it sometimes, 'as a well-meaning joke'. It is important to point out that while this might sound an overly critical statement, it typified Oris' frankness. Not even friendship could make him temper his critical forthrightness. His review of Kunle Afolayan's *The CEO*, he once told me, cost him his friendship with Kunle. He obviously did not regret his approach to film reviews. In his world, a critic's job is not to pander to the filmmaker's ego. It could be said that he would rather lose friends than impair his artistic integrity.

In what might have been an oblique response to Oris, Onyeka posted Brendan Behan's taunt of critics on his Facebook page:

'Critics are like Eunuchs in a harem; they know how it's done, they've seen it done every day, but they are unable to do it themselves.'

I suspected it was Onyeka's device for shrugging off irksome criticism. It was important, after all, to always appear the Teflon Don he considered himself.

'When I was looking for money, who gave me any? Now they want to be experts on how to make a documentary.'

It is easy to perceive that everyone, particularly creative people, are sensitive to censuring of their works. They might not voice their feelings, but long for everyone to acclaim their products.

On a certain morning in Lagos, Onyeka and I left our hotel for the Federal Palace Hotel on Victoria Island. We were going to attend the Lights Camera Africa Film Festival. He suddenly asked our taxi driver to stop at a supermarket on Ogudu road, near the by-pass that cuts into the Third Mainland Bridge. He bought Kargol wine, emptying that beverage into a coffee jug which bore HARVARD University in bold print. Onyeka told me he was afraid of being totally sober at the screening of his film. I had never seen him so tense.

I tried to brace him. 'But you've shown this film in Harvard. You've shown it in Ohio. You've shown

117

it in Harare. I think Nigerians love things that have already had fair reception overseas. They'll love your documentary, even if it was shit,' I said, as we moved along the wine racks in the supermarket. As he had opened and emptied his first bottle of Kargol wine into a coffee jug, he asked me to open the second bottle so that we could sip it on our way to the festival. By the time we reached the Federal Palace Hotel we were tipsy, having gulped down the entire contents of the bottle.

I recall that at the check-out till in the supermarket, the cashier had recognized him. 'You! Aren't you supposed to be in America?' Onyeka is now used to such acknowledgements. People continually come up to say they knew him from Facebook, and liked him. He had not at first realized how many people knew and followed his Facebook write-ups. One evening, as we were having drinks with Flavour's manager Benjamin Omesiete at Fahrenheit Hotel, he said: 'Onyeka, whenever I log into Facebook every morning, I just go straight to your profile to see what you've been talking about.' It was a confession that drew hearty laughter, and, I suspect, roused pride in Onyeka.

At the supermarket that day, he responded to the young girl's question: 'I came back to Nigeria yesterday, *Nne m*,' and, after a while, added with a cheeky smile, 'I came down so we could get married.' The girl was greatly tickled.

She checked out our purchases. She was about to tell Onyeka that he had overpaid, when he said: 'Yes, I overpaid by 1,000. Keep it.'

As soon as the cab stopped at the venue, we saw Ugoma Adegoke, founder and host of the LCA film festival. It had rained the previous night, and the well-tended vegetation at the Federal Palace was green, lush, and diffused a blissful coolness. Onyeka and Ugoma hugged and Onyeka handed her a bottle of wine, congratulating her for bringing about such a huge event. Onyeka told me that the film festival was in its fifth year, and I could only wonder how she had managed to run it successively. I looked at Ugoma, young, beautiful and energetic, who tried to chat to me in French when Onyeka told her my name. My French is dismal! Ashamed of my limited French, I slipped out of the conversation.

The viewing hall featured an orderly arrangement of white-covered chairs, the dim lights at the edges of the ceiling bestowing a perfect shade. It was hard not to think of Ugoma as a masterly organizer. I wondered how she had found the funds and personnel to host an event so grand, held in that swank hotel, with all the big names in film criticism present, and succeeded in providing so well for the crowd that came. The Federal Palace was definitely not a middling or lowly establishment!

I do not know if it was deliberate or sheer happenstance that the showing of Onyeka's film was scheduled for 6.30 pm. Although it was a Saturday, fixing it for that time enabled people to attend to their day's business and reach the venue in time to see it. The film was consequently guaranteed a much larger audience than those shown earlier. The hall was duly thronged by 6.30 pm. I had been outside chatting to acquaintances.

When I entered the hall, I was amazed at the numbers present. Onyeka had announced on his Facebook page that his film would be screened in Nigeria, and that he would attend the event. Although I expected that announcement to draw people, I was still surprised at the crowd I beheld. I again reflected later that Onyeka's personality did much to boost interest in his products. Many who had scant interest in Flora Nwapa would have come just to meet Onyeka.

Onyeka's personality, at least as perceived on social media, is contradictory. From the angle of the blogosphere, he is both penny-plain and mysterious, dominant and vulnerable. He could seem, simultaneously, a hero and a villain. Many, confronted with this intriguing quantity, would yearn for a physical encounter, an opportunity to plumb the complex persona. Whatever flaws Onyeka might have, he is not bland or commonplace.

The House of Nwapa documentary started with a lady sporting an Afro coiffure, eyes belching fire, screaming at the camera:

> 'We will never go back to Nigeria. Biafra will not be defeated. We will fight to the last man.'

With that, the hall fell into tense silence, everyone's eyes trained on the screen. I looked around the hall to know where Onyeka sat, and spotted him somewhere at the extreme left of the front row, still holding his coffee jar, the contents of which no one would have guessed.

The documentary gripped the hall. The only discernible sounds were heartbeats, with occasional bursts of laughter. So enthralled were viewers that many did not seem to know when it was over. Contrary to Onyeka's fears, the Q&A session was more like a feting than an interrogation. There were far more acclamatory effusions than criticisms.

'I was so nervous,' Onyeka told me later. 'I only began to relax when people started laughing during the interview. A girl next to me said "*oh, look at him struggling with his crutches*" in one of the places where I interviewed Ezenwanyi. She didn't know it was me sitting next to her. It was beautiful.' Shaibu Husseini, a judge of the African Movie Academy Awards, was full of praise for the work. So too was the legendary photographer, Fiofiri, who held Onyeka's hand that night, and lauded his film.

Back at the hotel, Onyeka told me he had just discovered something: there were online interactions about the film by people he knew. At first, I failed to grasp his drift, but soon learned he was curious as to why those people had not come to greet him after the screening. 'So why didn't they?' I asked him.

'I think they are disappointed that people enjoyed it,' he said, 'If it was an awful film, they would have come to console me, and tell me how life is sometimes like that, and that my next film would be better. Ogbuide has disappointed them!'

I swallowed hard, and said in humorous sarcasm:

'Or perhaps they just wanted to rush home after a long day, trying to beat traffic, maybe?'

'Mitt, I know what I'm saying,' he insisted.

What could not be taken away from Onyeka that night was his happiness. He was rapturous. He remained glued to his laptop, revelling in the praises that streamed forth on social media. Later that night, his phone beeped. Someone important had sent a message. He had totally forgotten to invite a close friend. It was Seun Kuti. Seun was in Lagos, had not known of the screening, and was displeased that he only learned of it social media.

Onyeka's joy was momentarily dampened by Seun's message. He scratched the partings in his hair, incredulous at his grievous oversight. 'But how did this happen?' He turned to look at me. 'How did I forget to invite Seun Kuti? And I used two of his songs for the film's soundtrack. Seun Kuti is really not happy, *Nna m*. God! But me, I don't want to feel bad today o!'

I urged him not to brood. 'It's a big day for you. You and Seun Kuti are too close for him to hold any grudges anyway.' As I left the room for my own room, I knew my soothing would not end his fretting. I knew what friendship meant to him, and Seun Kuti, as Onyeka would tell anyone who cared to listen, was one of the most genuine people he had ever met.

As for me, should I voice a verdict on *The House of Nwapa*, I would repeat the words of Ikhide, who called it 'a labor of love' where 'you ended up grinning through it all…sometimes for reasons other than the literary.'

9

AMBASSADOR GHANASHYAM

On the day I arrived in Abuja for preparations for the Diplomatic Jazz Night that would be held the following day at the Indian High Commission, I found Onyeka looking unwell. His face was swollen, his eyes weary and indicative of persistent insomnia. His habitual exuberance was absent. He had longed to give the Abuja diplomatic community an unforgettable show, but the goal had begun to appear unattainable. Our plans had looked good, but projections often looked good on paper until life's realities intruded.

As soon as I sauntered into his hotel room, I said, "*Nna*, you're not looking good, but take it easy." I had just seen the room arrangements in the hotel, and observed that people were paired up in rooms. I knew it was an unusual practice for Onyeka. He would typically allocate a room to every individual, and pick up their meal bills, even if they chose to eat ten times daily. I needed no one to tell me we were in a financial fix at the worst possible moment. As Onyeka and I continued to chat, a waiter knocked on the door to present Onyeka with a bill for five hundred naira, being Fanta drunk by one of the artistes. Onyeka shook his head and remarked, 'They can't even pay for their own Fanta. All these people that call themselves artistes.'

I was minded to tell him that he should have planned the event on a more modest scale, considering that none of our letters to corporate bodies received positive responses. I had drafted all the letters, and there were about fifteen. Half of the addressees were Onyeka's personal friends who occupied corporate executive positions in the firms we sought to reach. Those personal contacts were the only addressees who troubled to reply to us, and all made excuses or expressed regrets. I had become extremely apprehensive at that stage. However, I knew that Onyeka's unflinching faith in his own ability to overcome towering odds would lead us either to success or crushing disgrace.

The Abuja event was our second edition of the Diplomatic Jazz Night, and Onyeka was keen to surpass even the impressive debut at the Italian Consulate in Lagos. He also longed to make a certain man proud. He was Mr. Ghanashyam, India's Ambassador to Nigeria. His tenure had just ended and Onyeka wished the Jazz Night to be a personal farewell tribute to him.

When I settled into the sofa in the room and helped myself to a glass of the Johnny Walker black label whiskey on the table, Onyeka gave me dismaying news. Jyoti Goho, the maverick Indian Jazz Artist we were expecting, could not come after all. He was supposed to come with his son, Sourabh, which would have cost us at least ten thousand dollars or more. 'I met the Manager of Sterling Bank Abuja; the Ambassador sent me to him. But it was a little too late to plan for their visas.'

Onyeka might have suspected at some stage that I objected to the grand scale on which he conceptualized the event, and felt it was the cause of the disappointments we were having. He was also finding it a struggle to pay the bills of performing artistes. Artistes could be impatient or abrupt. If their comfort was not guaranteed, they were swift to abandon a project. We had also not hired a band to enable the performers to rehearse, and lacked money to do so. These were discouraging factors for a show scheduled for performance the following day.

'You know, I hadn't seen a total stranger accept me the way he, Mr. Ghanashyam did. I have to find a way to make this happen,' Onyeka said, tapping his feet on the marble floor and staring at the wall in front of him. 'He opened his heart, and his doors to me,' Onyeka said. It was his manner of explaining why he had taken enormous risks to honour the diplomat with a grand farewell.

'I had gone to the High Commission on a certain day to see the Defence Attache, Captain Marwaha when

I bumped into this grey-haired fellow standing by the door. I greeted him. And then he said, "How are you? I like your hair and your attire. What do you do?"

'I said, "I am a teacher and writer. And I teach in India."

'He said, 'Tell me what the titles of your books are?'

'I said I had a new book and that I could get him a copy from the car which had brought me, which was standing outside.'

'I went out to get the book and when I returned, some young man there said the High Commissioner asked him to lead me into his office. 'It was a surreal moment. I had all along been speaking to the High Commissioner and had no idea. He was easily the most unassuming man in the world.

'He offered me tea and asked me to sign the book in his name.

'When I emailed him about the jazz night, he said, "Come to the office so that we can have a meeting." At that meeting, he called together other staff of the high commission, and then asked Mr. M.S. Kanyal, the Chancellor, to give me all the assistance I needed for the event.

'You see,' Onyeka concluded, 'this is why this thing cannot fail.'

The next morning, we hired the band and stage paraphernalia, saved in the last second by a friend in Abuja, who gave Onyeka a five-hundred thousand Naira loan. Onyeka built strategic friendships which came in handy in such moments of need. When all seemed grim and lost, there would be an ace up his sleeve.

The following morning, before 10 am, I asked Onyeka if he needed me to assist with anything. I always had to do this with him, for he almost never asked for help. You had to put yourself forward and request to assist, or he carried on alone. That morning, like many occasions in his life, he appeared a man trying to balance an avalanche on his sagging shoulders. While the band impasse had been remedied, other crucial hurdles were yet to be surmounted. Printing of the programme leaflets for the day, getting the flex banner for the occasion done, and effective coordination of the performing artistes for the evening, all awaited execution.

'OK, can you stay at the High Commission and monitor how things are going over there?' he finally said, after I insisted on his assigning a task to me, so that he would not have to be responsible for all aspects of preparation, and possibly disintegrate at a crucial moment.

By the time I arrived at the High Commission that morning, rehearsals were underway. Orliam came first with his band members, and took up nearly three hours on the spin. Orliam exemplified virtuosity, never playing with a band crew that was not his, and watching his rehearsals felt like leafing through the trashed works of a genius poet. There were incomplete parts; it seemed like scraps of a gorgeous symphony. By the time the internationally acclaimed flutist, Tee-Mac Iseli, arrived for his own rehearsal, the morning sun had so intensified that I feared its rays would scorch or scar the flutist's light and gleaming skin.

I introduced myself to him as the communications director of the Diplomatic Jazz Night, and told him how pleased I was to have finally met him. Before then, I had on several occasions heard Onyeka extol Tee Mac Iseli. The cordial introduction however, did not stop him grumbling over the weather, the enervating rehearsal under the scorching sun, and the lack of better all-round coordination.

'Logistics,' I pleaded. 'We are facing issues of logistics and our financial resources are already overstretched.' He was not pacified.

'If you want to plan an event, you need three things,' he opined, touching the sides of his eye glass and looking me straight in the eye. 'Number one: money. Number two: money. And number three: money.' It is possible I would have found those words deflating, if I was not still lost in his legend. He quickly added, 'But I'm here for Onyeka. I love Onyeka. That's why I'm here.'

As the fiery evening sun mellowed into twilight, the beauty of the outdoor event lawn became radiantly evident. The arena, decorated by the network giant, Airtel, came alive in all the colours of India. The perimeter fence was draped in the country's colours, as were the seat coverings and ribbons fastened to the open roof of the stage. They looked gorgeous in the evening lights.

At exactly 6:30 pm, the anticipated night commenced with poetry performances by Chika Onwuasoanya, and the award-winning poet, Ikeogu Oke. Ikeogu, who won the NLNG Prize for Literature 3 years later, died tragically of cancer the following year. Other artistic performances followed. There were John Bethel and Lugi. Afterwards came Edge, Asikey, who won the *Best Female Artist in Inspirational Music* at the All Africa Music Awards in 2017, and the incredible young violinist, Victor Azuka. Orliam presently thrilled with his arresting voice, but Ugo Stevenson, Tee-Mac and Yinka Davies gave the night's show-stopping performances.

Oby Ezekwesili, Fmr. Minister of Education arrives at the event with her husband, Pastor Ezekwesili, exchanging greetings with Ambassador Ghanashyam and Onyeka.

I should describe the experience of watching and hearing Tee-Mac on stage. He did many things with the flute. I had seen flutes in my childhood, but had never seen one like his. I knew of the wooden flute, an important instrument in pre-colonial Igbo society because it was used by town criers to summon people to meetings at the village square, or at chiefs' compounds. An *ogbu-oja*, the typical flutist in Igbo society, belonged in a league of wonderful storytellers. They used idioms and proverbs in their tales, accompanied with flourishes of their stirring instrumental music. My knowledge of the flute was therefore limited to the wooden flute, while I had little interest in the modern flute or music from its instrumentation. Tee-Mac blew everyone away! In fact, we had not then noticed that the amazing Yinka Davies was present, until Tee Mac's playing reached a stage where she could no longer contain her delight.

One more surprise remained to be savored that night. It was Ugo Stevenson, the Igbo High-Life artiste who shot up the fervor in the venue to its topmost peak. Ugo had a distinctive manner on stage. He was a mobile entertainment house, singing from his soul, displaying dance moves that were absolutely inimitable. They were varied, spontaneous, sometimes staccato, and utterly enthralling. From where I stood, I saw the members of the Diplomatic Corps in Nigeria, including the US Ambassador, James F. Entwistle, and the Ukrainian Ambassador, Dr. Valerii Aleksandruk, moving their heads to Ugo's rhythms. Suddenly, Dr. Oby Ezekwesili, formerly Nigeria's Minister of Education and former Deputy Director of the World Bank, sprang to her feet, gripped by the music, and danced away. It was a gladdening moment, as Onyeka leant towards me to ask: 'You remember what she told us when she arrived?'

'What?' I asked.

'That she wouldn't stick around for long as she had other engagements. The show is almost over and she's still here enjoying it.'

Dr Oby stayed until the very end of the show, then called Onyeka aside to say '*Nna, jisie ike*. This idea of yours is amazing.'

Those were precious and uplifting words, the balm Onyeka had needed for the past week, when he was beset with the strains of planning and organizing. He had longed for support from someone who could appreciate what he was trying to achieve with the Jazz Night. If there had been no other encouragement, he would have been heartened by a sincere: 'I can't support financially this time, but please let me know when the next one is coming up.' He would have been glad to be encouraged by people and leaders he respected, even if the funding was not immediately available. None of these hopes had materialized, and he had been forlorn in the weeks before the event. It had been his irrepressible will, a steely core, the last spark of irrational courage within him that carried him through the project against all the obstacles he encountered.

As he gave his speech that night, perhaps remembering what a strenuous process he had undergone and sad at the imminent departure of his friend Mr Ghanashyam, Onyeka was emotional and he sobbed.

Onyeka, presenting a gift to Amb. Ghanashyam at the Diplomatic Jazz Night, Indian High Commission, Abuja. January, 2016.

'Thank you, Your Excellency,' Onyeka began, in brisk and even tones that no one could have imagined would eventually quaver. 'You have been a father to me. You opened your doors to me in a way nobody else had ever done. You have made my dream come true. I started the Diplomatic Jazz Night as a way of introducing the Nigerian people to the Foreign Missions we have in the country, in order to improve their understanding of us, to challenge their imaginations of our people, many of which are not palatable. And I thought, "what if we could do this through music, through Jazz, because music unites people, and has no language?" We can relate to a song whose language we do not understand; that is the power of music. Your simplicity and humility are so charming, and within a short time I have learnt a lot from you.'

At this point, Onyeka's voice faltered, the sadness of parting overcoming him. Someone handed Onyeka a wrapped parcel which gift he presented to the Ambassador. 'I wish you would stay in Nigeria and never leave,' Onyeka said, unveiling the present by pulling a string from its cover. It was a beautiful portrait of the Ambassador by David Osagie. Onyeka's tears were now flowing, the hall falling into poignant silence. 'I know you'll leave tomorrow, and I'm giving you this, to say thank you for everything. Thank you for saving a dream that would have died if I had taken it to a Nigerian.'

Beside me was Ikeogu, who leant close to say, 'That last part is not a very brilliant idea. How can he say such a thing about us? He's your friend. I believe he listens to you. He's such a determined person and a go-getter, but he needs to tone down on the way he says things. I like his spirit, but you should try and talk to him.' Of course, the irony was not lost on me. The aim of the Jazz Night had been to redeem the image of Nigeria and Nigerians in foreigners' opinions. To imply that Nigerians would have killed the venture at its inception had it been left to them, was neither prudent nor necessary.

Was the irony lost on Onyeka? Was he merely overwhelmed by emotion, and spoke out of a bursting heart? Did the initial travails he suffered in the build-up to the event cut too deep? I'll never know any of these. I never raised the topic, despite promising Ikeogu that I would advise Onyeka to be more cautious and tactful in the future. I knew Onyeka better than he; and I knew that friends who were too critical and less understanding of him, irked him. In my own case, it was not fear of losing his friendship that stopped me from holding that conversation, but my understanding of his character. He was someone who wished to come to the truth on his own terms, who loved to hold up a mirror to his face and reflect on things and experience his own epiphanies, away from the judgmental gaze and counsel of friends. However, when he spoke on stage that night, I was convinced that he meant every word he uttered about Nigerians' penchant for dismissing projects that would not bring them immediate or foreseeable benefits. He would repeat those words a hundred times even if he were tied to a stake and facing a smoking gun. Onyeka often felt that others' cautionary advice about his ambitious projects tended to obscure his vision and limit his mind. He felt such advice tried to package him in a skin that was not his. He would rather listen to the voices in his head, remaining the proverbial masquerade that beat its own drum. He was, in his imagination, udo *akpu enyi*! An elephant that could not be led on a leash.

10

THE BEATING

When I stepped into Onyeka's hotel room in Owerri on the morning of 28th January, 2017, I found him in bed looking frail and battered. There had been no indications of illness when we spoke on the phone three days earlier, or even on the morning that I left Umuahia for Owerri. Because our phone conversations were usually brief, it was impossible to discern that he was undergoing acute physical pain.

It was our first meeting in about 7 months, since he assumed his research fellowship at Ohio University, Athens, USA. I had extended my hand for greetings, but he failed to move and kept his curled-up posture in bed. I said, 'Hey, I'm trying to give you a handshake.'

He raised his right hand to shake mine, but it swung above mine. He did the same, a second and a third time. A swing, and a miss. It became apparent by this time that he was probably not seeing my hand.

'Army people beat me silly in Abuja two days ago. I can't see, *Nna m. Ndi a kukasiri m ahu*[8] yesterday. My whole face is swollen.' He held up the ROB mentholated balm in his left hand. 'I've been applying this to my face to see if the swelling will go down a bit.'

We were supposed to be on our way to the *Igba Nkwu*[9] ceremony of Laura Ikeji, Linda Ikeji's younger sister scheduled to be just an hour after my arrival. She was getting married to Ogbonna Kanu, younger brother to former Nigeria and Arsenal FC star, Kanu Nwankwo.

'I wish I could just lie here and not go. But Laura isn't going to forgive me. How could I explain my absence? I bought my flight ticket back to Nigeria the day after she told me she was getting married. I'll be there. Let her just see me. I'll put on a sunshade and cover my eyes,' he said, with a defiance that was inspiriting for everyone who had come to the hotel to accompany him on the trip.

As I sat there, I could imagine the savagery with which those army officers must have put dispensed every single punch that struck him. It is true that he is tall, with locks so thick and long look like a lion's mane. However, he was frailer than he might immediately appear. His upper frame was not very muscular. No blows, ferocious as he described them, would have encountered effective resistance.

---

8 Those people battered my body
9 'Wine-carrying' – traditional wedding ceremony

I had seldom seen him so vulnerable, helpless and desolate.

'My father didn't know I came to Nigeria. He would have tried to stop me. He is still in Ohio with my mother. I called him only when I arrived in Abuja. You know, he would have been telling me... I told you about that godforsaken place.'

'I haven't seen you make a Facebook post in the last three days,' I said, 'and I was starting to wonder, because it was so unlike you.'

'I can't. I can't type anything. I can't use my laptop. My body still feels sore. My hands are shaking. I've been waiting for you to come so you can help me write something.'

'Sure, why not?' I replied, unzipping my bag and pulling out my laptop from its pouch.

He began:

I arrived Nigeria on the 24ᵗʰ of January, 2017. Two days later, on the 26ᵗʰ of January, 2017, around 1am, about 10 or more members of a joint-task force including army cadets, policemen and civil defence corps descended on me and beat me up so brutally, my body still feels sore.

I had arrived at the entrance of my hotel in Crystal Palace, Garki, Abuja. I came in with three others. And suddenly, we saw a lady run past us into the hotel's lobby. She looked terrified. She fell there, screaming, pleading, on the floor. Close behind her, we saw someone come and drag her out of the hotel. This man was viciously dragging this lady on the concrete floor that stood between the lobby and the exit of the hotel.

The person wasn't wearing a uniform, and so, for a moment, we wondered if this might be a rapist. So I stepped out to ask the man to let the woman go. As the man stopped in his tracks, the woman held my hand and began to scream: 'Help me. Make dem no carry me, I get pikin.'[10]

The man was adamant and continued to drag her on the floor. So, I followed them up to the road. There I met a soldier whom the plain-clothed officer exchanged a few words with. When I saw the army personnel was with them, I started pleading with the soldier.

In the process of pleading, more people in uniforms arrived, about 10 or more. And a few began to ask, 'What is your business in the matter, she is an ashawo.'[11]

At this point, another officer arrived, I think the patrol commander. He inquired what was going on and they explained to him. He too told me "Oga, mind your business o."[12]

'These are the people who are supposed to protect us,' I said, out of frustration and to their hearing.

After that, one of them asked 'Who are you?'

'I am a teacher, sir,' I said. 'Look at my ID.' I pointed to the University of Ohio ID hanging down on my neck.

This probably may have angered them. And most of them

---

10 Don't let them take me. I have a child.

11 Prostitute

12 Boss, mind your business o.

began to say: 'mind yourself in this country o. Mind yourself in this country o.'

Before I could say anything else, they pounced on me. I was being beaten so brutally, if you were from afar, you'd think it was a punching bag being kicked. How do you defend against 10 men? Within minutes, I was blinded from the blows and kicks.

All the while, my friends were begging and pleading for them to let go of me. But even after they left me, I asked my friends to take me back to them, that I still wanted to talk to them. Frankly, at that point, I just wanted them to finish me.

When we got there, I said 'Look what you people have done to me, because I asked that you should let go of the woman you were violating?'

I think the soldiers probably got sick of me at that point, and commanded me to get into their bus, but if their bus was east, I was heading west. I was just following voices, as I still couldn't see properly at that point. I think they probably became frightened at that point, when I was heading in the wrong direction. My friends later told me that that was when they got into their trucks and fled.

My friends took me to the Garki National Hospital to see if I could get treatment for the eye. Of course, over there, Nigeria shows you much it has no value for human life. Instead of appreciating the urgency of the situation, they were asking me that I needed to register, take a card, and all those time-waiting processes, in a situation where I was bleeding in the eye and needed emergency attention. Finally, they told me there was no optometry doctor on seat and it would have to wait till morning.

My friends took me to eight different hospitals that they knew, and none of them were open. This was a journey that began around 2am, and we were on this long fruitless journey until 5am. Finally, we went to H-Medix in Wuse II so they could prescribe some drugs for me.

Such misfortune, for asking that a woman, who was being ruthlessly dragged on hard ground, whose blood was dripping all over the floor, should be let go. I think (I am not sure), they eventually left the woman. I had a meeting with the Norwegian Ambassador the next day, and I couldn't see either him or anyone I was speaking to. I was just hearing voices and responding. He couldn't believe his eyes.

Right now, I had to ask a good friend who arrived at my hotel this morning to help me transcribe this tale. Because my hands still feel numb, I can barely raise them, let alone do anything meaningful. My face has been swollen for the last 72 hours. I still cannot see properly. I think my left eye, the one that blood came out from, smells. I can smell it. I have to close the left eye with my palms to be able to see anything, or everything appears in a blur.

Later that day, we drove down to Nkwerre in a convoy of two cars, mine and Arinze's. Arinze is a friend of Onyeka's living in Owerri. With Onyeka in an all-black attire, complete with a long mafia jacket, all seven of us make our way to the ceremony. As we huddled through the clusters of people at the gates of the Ikeji compound, I heard the conversation of two policemen who were debating whether Onyeka was the groom. Finally, inside the compound, we heard one of the MCs announce to the delight of the seated guests that an international superstar had just arrived, and it was no other than the acclaimed Wyclef Jean. Some laughed, and others clapped. With his bead, cap and locks, Onyeka did look on that occasion like the Wyclef of the 90s.

In the living room, we saw MC Galaxy, Kanu Nwankwo, Segun Arinze, and a few other Nollywood people. Onyeka greeted the mother and father of the bride with whom he was closely acquainted. Everyone in our group, except me, then went outside. I sat alone at the dinner table in the sitting room, busying myself with my smart-phone. My crowd phobia had gathered momentum; the celebration outside felt to me like a commotion, a riot.

While I was there, I saw Laura appear with her suite of uniformed (*asoebi*-clad) young ladies, about to go outside to enact the traditional ritual of finding the bridegroom amongst a cluster of other men. A bubbly character from all indications, one could see Laura dance *shoki* right there, in response to the music playing outside the house. The Nollywood actor, Francis Duru, who was the Master of Ceremonies, came in to ask Laura if there was a special song she would like to dance to as she made her regal entry into the compound from the house.

'No,' she said. 'No particular song. I'm fine with anything.'

As she moved towards the door, I heard a loud 'Onyeka!' Laura and Onyeka hugged, and took a 'selfie' as she thanked him for honoring her invitation. 'I'm back in Owerri this evening,' she told him. 'Try and come to our hotel. Lots to talk about.'

From where I sat inside the house, I could hear the hysteric voices in the crowd, similar to a home team scoring an injury time winner on their home turf. And then I could tell that the bride had found her man, presented him with the ceremonial drink, sealing the rites of marriage. It was at that stage that we left the venue, whilst the towering speakers boomed and numerous cheerful people surrounded the couple.

When we were outside the compound, Onyeka told us that he needed to go to Oguta to see Ogbuide, the chief priestess of the river goddess. *Ezenwanyi* as he fondly called her, was one person he could not afford not to visit.

'But you know, I've been thinking, Nna. How come Ogbuide did not save you from this kind of beating though?' I asked to the amusement of everyone, prompting a few concurring nods.

Onyeka paused for a moment, as though asking himself the same question, but eventually said, 'Well, it couldn't save me.' Everyone laughed again.

Self-portrait showing the battered right eye in February, 2017

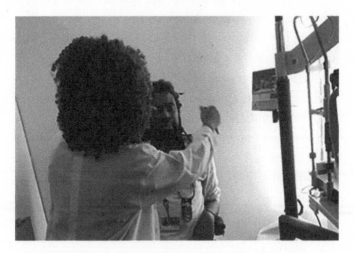

Receiving treatment in Abuja, a week after the beating.
February, 2017

He knew my question was not aimed at deriding the reputed powers of the goddess. I was merely expressing my curiosity. Besides, I had believed what he told me about his accident in Abuja, 6 months earlier. As he headed for the Abuja International Airport, some car had smashed into the taxi carrying him. Onyeka had told me he emerged unscathed, because Ogbuide was protecting her own. Of course, so absolute and unwavering was his faith in Ogbuide, that he had advised it would be to my benefit to visit the chief priestess on my own.

'I don't believe these things would work for me,' I had demurred. 'You know, I'm just happy with the Catholic boy I am. Nobody knows whether I come to church on Sunday or not. I don't have things I'd have to stop doing, like giving up sex, mandatory offering to one's supreme deity and the like. I'm a lazy person when it comes to religion and worship. The fewer rules I have to worry about, the better.'

He did not raise the topic again, but he knew I was comfortable with his voodoo beliefs, which he practiced with pride and dedication.

As we approached Oguta, Onyeka prophesied that what happened to those who tried to 'send' paralysis to him when he was in Peru, would befall the soldiers who had belaboured him. They would feel the force of Ogbuide's wrath. The river goddess never let anyone who harmed her son go free, without exacting retribution. Ogbuide, Onyeka told me, never struck the innocent. If he had transgressed, Ogbuide would not have acted on his behalf. He had not wronged those soldiers, and they had unleashed their savagery on him because he could neither defend himself nor return their blows. Now, they would all suffer a hundred times the brutality they had inflicted on him. He pronounced: 'Every single one of them will suffer, so much, they would pray to die.'

He paused for a while and asked, 'Meanwhile, what are you still doing in this country?'

I replied that I too was sick of the country and would soon leave for my doctorate studies. He worried that I did not exhibit any sense of urgency about it. 'You know, there's so much ageism here. So much disdain from old people towards young Nigerians, especially if they are looking successful." A paused. "Do you know Aboyeji has left Nigeria for good?' he asked, now getting emotional. 'He has moved all of his things to San Francisco, California. That's the guy that brought Zuckerberg to Nigeria. But he landed at the Lagos International Airport a few weeks ago, and men of EFCC and the DSS (Secret Service) picked him up and took him to Abuja. They said he must explain what he told Zuckerberg to make him dole out $27 million funding to his company. Can you imagine? These people have their brains so fried up, they don't know software developers are ruling the world.'

We soon resumed our conjecture over what might have motivated the army men's brutality. Onyeka suspected that his brandishing of his Ohio University ID might have roused their envious fury. I told him that our country still suffered the hangover of our militarized governance between the first and the third republics. Nigerian military personnel have a long history of hostility to academics, intellectuals, outspoken writers, journalists and critics. I recalled how people like Abdul Mahmud (known in his student days as 'Obemeta'), Obiwu Iwuanyanwu, and Olu Oguibe, to name a few, were thrown into prison for confronting the Buhari/Idiagbon regime in 1984-85. Even Wole Soyinka suffered a similar fate in 1967, and would spent three whole years behind military bars.

'God!' Onyeka screamed, patting his forehead with his right palm, 'Why didn't I call Wole Soyinka after this happened? He would've made contact with top people in the military; he would have found out exactly who my attackers were.'

II

THE LAKE

The lake in Oguta, which has two colours – bluish green and greyish brown – has a powerful spiritual attraction for Onyeka. The water was his temple, a place where he went to bare his soul, to shed the accumulated weight and worries of living. The Oguta Lake restored the tranquillity of his mind. The Lake was the dwelling place of the water goddess, Ogbuide, who awaited and welcomed adherents. Onyeka believed in Ogbuide. She protected him from malignant foes, bestowed fame on him, and although she did not make him rich, shielded him from lack.

'When I went to see Ezewanyi, the priestess of Ogbuide, she asked me to choose between fame and wealth. I chose fame.' Onyeka once wrote this in an update on his Facebook page. It was one of those write-ups which thousands of his followers read and failed to comprehend. Some might suspect it was a mere jest, perhaps sheer sarcasm. 'The talkative has said a new one,' many would have said and shrugged, then scrolled towards other matters.

I, too, wondered if he wrote that in seriousness. I pushed it to the back of my mind. As time went by, however, and he grew more familiar to me, I began to see that certain chains of events in his life, some aspects of his life's journey, made that declaration plausible, if not utterly convincing.

I have sometimes pondered that claim. Is he famous, then? Well, this would depend on how one chooses to define fame. He is at least famous enough to be known by your favourite actor, your favourite artiste, federal minister, ambassador, ex-president, Nobel Laureate, Man Booker laureate. Onyeka is famous enough to have your most admired superstar on speed dial.

Is he wealthy? This, too, depends on what one defines as wealth, and if one did it by the Nigerian standard, the answer would be 'no.' From what I knew, he had no tangible assets. While he travelled to several international destinations every year, he had no savings whatsoever. Perhaps he is not supposed to. Was that one of the conditions for his attainment of fame? I had no idea. As I also know, he has no house of his own, neither does he reside in any of Abuja's or Lagos' posh neighbourhoods. Furthermore, Onyeka occupies no executive position in any company or firm, where he earns a decent five or six figure salary, as top bankers or company MDs do. Given these considerations, it may be fair to speculate that he was actually granted his choice: *fame over wealth.*

Onyeka on the shore of the Oguta Lake

In any case, while he worshipped the goddess with fervent devotion, he pursued his dreams with tenacity. I have been moved to ask him whether he was not exaggerating the goddess' influence in his success. Once, we arrived together at a hotel and settled into separate rooms. When I asked if I could come over later for a brief chat, he said we would talk the following day.

'What happened?' I asked in the morning.

'I was burning candles,' he explained. 'I don't like the people closest to me coming into my room when I burn candles.' I did not ask why. I tend not to pry into others' religion and spirituality.

I recall other stories Onyeka told me, of people

who owed their success, riches or wealth to Ogbuide. Some of them failed later to show proper appreciation to the goddess. They failed to make required visits to Ezenwanyi, to presents gifts for the deity and venerate the goddess in her holy place. Those ungrateful people, Onyeka told me, later stumble into misfortunes. He once spoke of a famous Nollywood star who was so desperate to get married to a certain hunk in the industry that she slept at the shrine for three nights. In the end, she got the man, and then reneged on her duty to return to the shrine to render thanks. The marriage was over in less than three years.

I cannot confirm the merits of the story, but I do not necessarily doubt it either. They accorded with the observations of the German Professor of Anthropology, Sabine Jell-Bahlsen, about the Water Goddess. Sabine noted in her book that Ogbuide had binary propensities, which meant that while she was capable of changing one's destiny for the better, she was also capable of permanently wrecking a life. She would heal, bestow wealth and protect the lives of those who reverenced her, but she could inflict mortal calamity.

Onyeka had an abiding faith in his spiritual creed, and could go as far as proselytising, even if tangentially. He has at various times posted pictures of himself in the shrine with Ezenwanyi on social media. He called himself an unashamed voodooist, a worshipper of the Water Goddess, and was ready with rejoinders for those who dubbed him an idol worshipper. In defence of his religion and mode of worship, on 11ᵗʰ November, 2016, he made an emphatic announcement on his Facebook account:

> 'I'm a proud worshipper of Ogbuide, the Goddess of Oguta Lake. I have done Jesus Christ in the past. Spent six years of my life in the seminary. I don't regret worshipping Jesus from the day I was born and forced into it by my overzealous parents. I also don't blame people who worship Jesus Christ. I don't condemn them. For now, Jesus Christ is not for me. Since I respect and cherish Christians, I want everybody on my Facebook to show me some respect when I share pictures from the shrine or where I perform rituals.'

This was a public affirmation of his creed, in response to critics who wrote to him on social media, drumming up Jesus Christ to him, preaching about his need for repentance, and being 'born-again.' Onyeka's response failed to deter many of those commentators.

Once, a friend innocently asked me, 'This your friend, this thing he's doing, isn't it paganism?'

'It depends on how you see it,' I responded, 'given that Muslims in the North of the country call Christians like us *Kafirs*, or unbelievers. I think everyone is a pagan to someone who isn't worshipping their own God. The same way most of us Christians don't think

Muslims worship the true God and will most likely not make heaven. They, too, I suppose, are pagans in our estimation.' Lost for words, she shrugged and said, 'I know you'll always support him.'

Onyeka scooping water from the Lake to sluice his face

Onyeka, washing his face with water from the Lakeside

Whenever he returned to Nigeria from an overseas trip, he would fly to Owerri, then travel by road to Oguta, to the Lake. He would meet with the Ezenwanyi, presenting her with gifts of money, beautiful fabrics, and other such valuable items. He would then go to the shore of the lake to splash its water on his face. It was a hallowed ritual whenever he was in Nigeria, a duty methodically executed in all its aspects.

Rumours have circulated that the face-washing ritual has brought Onyeka the love of many. It has been said that his charm, his ability to make people do his bidding, is the yield of magical powers derived from his face-rinsing at the lake. Given my closeness to him, this allegation is nonsensical. Onyeka has an effervescent, engaging personality. He is chatty, and can spin a cheeky joke out of the most mundane things. It would be ludicrous to imagine a deity could alter someone's personality to make them magically appealing to strangers.

For Onyeka, Oguta and its Lake dispensed inexhaustible bounties. I knew he visited the lake after the miscreants nearly beat him to death. He sought both succour and vengeance from Ogbuide. I drove him on that trip. It was also to the lake and shrine that we went when a car, believed to have been dispatched by his foes, rammed into the taxi conveying him to the Abuja International Airport at full speed.

'It happened just on the Lugbe-Airport Road Bridge,' he told me. 'I think the plan was to hit my own car with force and make it tip over from the bridge and crash-land. But I just watched the car screech to a slow halt after that. People gathered there chattering that they heard the impact and didn't expect the person sitting at the back would be alive. I was at the back. I just sat there motionless for about 20 minutes, trying to take all of that in, the force, the impact, the fact that I was unhurt. They acted like they had seen a ghost when I came out of the car. I simply took pictures of the ruined car, waved down another taxi, and continued my journey.' He told me he got a call from the priestess that someone was trying to get him killed; but he knew of a truth, that no one could kill the child of Ogbuide.

I also recall an occasion when I was in his hotel room, and six armed mobile policemen stormed into the room, demanding his passports and declaring him under arrest. This was at some lowly hotel in Ogudu, Ojota, Lagos State. They were accompanied by Mr James, an acquaintance of Onyeka's.

'Bring all your 6 passports,' they roared. A ludicrous order, to which he instantly replied, 'It is not here. It's with the embassy.'

'Why would your passports be at the Embassy?' one of them barked.

'I had to keep it there to prevent men like you from getting anywhere near it,' Onyeka sneered as he moved under his blanket, looking them in the eye. The confused men got into a huddle with Mr James who had brought them.

Mr James presently saw off his armed companions, then returned to rage: 'How can you have six passports filled with visas and you've been giving me stories about the Spanish visa you promised to do for me, even after paying you 500,000 naira?'

'But was that why you called the police on me? And asked them to go after my 6 passports, something I showed you while we were riding in the car yesterday? If it was about your money, why didn't you say so, and I'll refund you? It took you two weeks to get that money to me upon request. I'd simply have asked you to give me the same amount of time to come up with it. But my passports? Why come after my passports? You who have visited Ezenwanyi with me? You whom I actually cared about?' Weeks later, Onyeka told me that the priestess had called James to ask why he had acted as he did. Onyeka swore he never told the priestess of the incident, which of course is baffling. Whether this was true or not does not really matter to me; I have neither a way of confirming or disproving same. What I can attest to is that in his daily life, he considers Ogbuide and Ezenwanyi omnipresent forces, watching him intently, sometimes seeing ahead of him and warning him of impending danger.

Onyeka at the entrance of the dilapidated Oguta Lake Golf Course, built by writer Flora Nwapa

It may be necessary to add that Onyeka is bound to the lake, not only by religion and veneration of the Water Goddess, but also by his affinity with the land of Oguta. This was prompted by factors of which many people are unaware. Onyeka's mother was raised in Oguta, living there for her entire life before her marriage caused her relocation. Onyeka had also worked with Emeka Aseme, an Oguta indigene who made much money overseas, before returning to Oguta with plans of transforming the idyllic town into an enviable holiday resort. He built a hotel and a Western-style pub, intending to create similar pubs across the town. He contacted Onyeka, asking him to create a website for promoting Oguta as a holiday haven, then referred to him for funds to achieve that goal. A few weeks after work began on actualizing those plans, Emeka Aseme was kidnapped. Many days later, his lifeless body was found in a gutter, mangled and decomposing. Oguta is also hometown to Charles Oputa, a.k.a 'Charley Boy,' in whose audacious life many have seen parallels with Onyeka's. The insouciance, eccentricity, strikingly beringed fingers and startling garb, and the clout, might all be mentioned. Oguta was also the hometown of Flora Nwapa, the subject of Onyeka's Documentary film, *The House of Nwapa*. That documentary brought Onyeka one of his proudest accolades – a finalist for an African Academy Movie Award nomination for *Best Documentary Film*. For Onyeka, the lake was life, and Oguta was an eternal blessing.

12

DREAMS MAY COME TRUE BUT NEVER FREE

*G*iven all that my friend has been through so far in his young life, I must admit that I had wished this appraisal of his life to end on a triumphant note. I could say that this is the story of a 31-year-old Nigerian, who strives for greatness despite the inescapable drawbacks of being Nigerian. I might call this the story about a boy from Ezeoke Nsu, a little village in south-eastern Nigeria, who made a film that won him the Best Director Prize at the Newark International Film Festival in New Jersey. I would also add that his documentary, *The House of Nwapa*, was shortlisted for Africa's biggest film award, the AMAA. I could tell you that my friend has greater social capital than many people twice his age could even imagine. I might then mention that on the night he was arrested by EFCC on his return to Nigeria on 22nd January, 2018, he asked to be allowed one phone call. That call was to Wole Soyinka who, without asking what his offence might be, asked foremost human rights lawyer, Femi Falana, to work for his release. He was freed on that night, and spared the agonies of the police cell.

I could tell you that my friend, who dropped out of the University of Nigeria's Anthropology Department, has written and created works that made him an esteemed guest of top academic establishments around the world. He has been a research fellow in Harvard University, Ohio University, Manipur University India, and at the time of writing this, University of Johannesburg, South Africa. I could tell you that in this time, he has endeared himself to a dazzling array of globally revered cultural and creative icons, from Arundhati Roy and Wole Soyinka to Prof. Louis Gates Jr. and Zakes Mda, from Jane Elliot to Shobha Dee. If there were some personage or celebrity you sought to meet, my friend could take you to them, or connect you to someone who could make such an introduction happen. I watched his adroit interview with the former President, Olusegun Obasanjo, about the Biafran war, and the national figures that featured in that tragic conflict. Such is the breadth of his social capital and range of his network. However, while these attainments are impressive, they are only the icing on a cake crammed with private anguish.

This is why, in setting out these final pages, I made conscious efforts to suppress hagiographical urges.

My belief is that fidelity to the story, to events that impacted Onyeka's existence until this point, must not be discarded for a contrived, triumphant conclusion. There is little triumph in Onyeka's life. He flounders like everyone who gets up from bed each morning but cannot tell where their path will eventually lead. It is a life in which the false calculus of time and the dubious adrenaline of ambition have dealt him several blows. If the combination of these forces propelled him to great heights, it also left him exposed and vulnerable to gloomy consequences.

When I sat with Onyeka in his house in Auckland Park, Johannesburg, sometime in September 2019, I could see how embattled his life was. The bright spark from that encounter was that his mental health, which for some time had seemed imperilled, was now balanced.

'Here, my medical documents,' he said, pointing at the table in the centre of the sitting room. 'The last two weeks have been hell. I was beginning to hear all kinds of voices. My head has felt heavy, and I could barely sustain a train of thought without distraction and diversions.' Picking up the documents, I discovered that he had checked himself into a comprehensive psychotherapy programme at the Helen Joseph Hospital, Johannesburg. In the Nursing Notes was the following information:

Onyeka Nwelue
Patient. No. 010308

31 year old man received. Came alone in walking condition. Breathing well. Main component of depression pattern was diagnosed.

1. Depressive mood
2. Anhedonia
3. Changes in weight
4. Insomnia
5. Pscyhomotor retardation
6. Loss of energy + fatigue
7. Feelings of worthlessness
8. Suicidal ideations

'You know,' he began, after I had gone through all the medical transcripts, 'I poured out my heart to my shrink. I told her everything. Things I've never told you. She said the bulk of the trauma I suffered leading to this point was from my prison time in EFCC in Benin, not even from my accident. And I agree with her. Those people padlocked me. They gave me watery beans to eat. Their *Oga* told me, "Call your Wole Sonyinka na!" He was shocked that the same Wole Soyinka came through for me.'

Onyeka Nwelue and Wole Soyinka, on the set of Onyeka Nwelue Show (Available on Linda Ikeji TV)

When I met Onyeka in 2015, one of the first things I noticed was that he had a Savior Complex. He felt a need to assure all his friends that he could solve all their problems, or at least, make the best possible attempt to do so. As a result, he would introduce these friends to his network of important personalities. If some friend urgently needed to fly out of the country over a career or medical emergency, Onyeka would borrow if need be to purchase their ticket. What neither of us understood was that this tendency reflected a complex and unplumbed psychological dysfunction. This Savior Complex was neither natural nor born of compassion. It stemmed instead from a yearning to be a protective force in the lives of others. It was of course a longing that was self-imposed. He felt a need to earn their love and respect, which in hindsight, was neither necessary nor useful to him. Most times in fact, these caring gestures ended badly for him. Friends who were introduced to his exalted contacts proved uncouth or opportunistic, figuratively burning bridges for him and for themselves, turning his goodwill to resentment. Those whose dreams he sought to finance became veritable Oliver Twists, continually demanding more favours. When he refused to grant those inconsiderate demands, they turned angry and spiteful, of course forgetting his earlier generosity.

In any case, his emotional distress and subsequent scramble for treatment were caused mainly by his increasing debts, the hounding of creditors. These debts, I understood, were accumulated in two ways. The first were funds he borrowed from individuals which he found himself unable to refund within the agreed period. The second were ventures which failed. There was the case of his taking a loan of N6m naira from an individual to make the film, *Agwaetiti Obiuto* (Island of Happiness). He was certain that the film would be successful enough to earn international acclaim, or at least be so impressive that top film distributors would readily promote it in cinemas. He projected that the accrued earnings would repay his loan. This could be deemed at worst a naïve risk, and at best, an entrepreneur's misplaced optimism. It was indicative of his adventurous spirit, but also a reflection of his inability to engage in worst-case scenario analysis. He mostly did not consider the consequences of failure. That apart, another activity that got him into debt was his travel agency company. The business initially was remarkably successful, making him one of the most sought-after people for visas to Nigerians' favourite destinations. At some stage, however, the exigencies of business imposed a financial burden which had not been envisaged. You could convince clients that their visas would be issued, and they in turn would pay for the service, sometimes handsomely. Convinced of a positive outcome, you might proceed to spend their money on solving your own problems. However, visas, especially for those with Nigerian passports, do not have guaranteed outcomes. Clients might lie in their application forms, a Consular officer might not be convinced of an applicant's genuineness, someone's enemy could have written to the Embassy with damning allegations against them. Any of these factors, and many others, could cause the refusal of an application. When that happens, the person assisting with obtaining the visa becomes an enemy, and is vilified as a fraudster, a scammer. Aggrieved clients could go as far contacting the police or EFCC to arrest the person. Every travel agent in Nigeria would understand this chain of events.

That was how Onyeka found himself in a situation where his life in Nigeria became akin to a fugitive's. His creditors wanted him imprisoned until he paid his debts, and his visa clients clamored for similar treatment for him. There was, in fact, an incident when he was called on the phone repeatedly. He avoided taking the calls. The caller then sent an SMS urging him to answer because he was being summoned to a shrine. That was the first of repeated attempts by creditors to recover their debts by fetish scare ruses. When these tactics failed, those he owed began to file various incriminating petitions against him with the EFCC. Some of their reasons were as absurd as they were sadistic. If breach of a loan agreement were grounds for a petition, alleging that he engaged in human trafficking or obtaining-by-trick (OBT) were both malicious and untrue.

There is a tendency for people to derive gratuitous pleasure from heckling and humiliating those with whom they are aggrieved. To me, this seemed pronounced in Nigerian society. I saw that my friend's frequent brushes with the law, which I concluded to be partly accidental and partly self-inflicted, not only robbed him of sleep, but subjected him to intense mental strain. Hounded for long spells and without respite, Onyeka began to seek a permanent solution to his challenges.

Once, he considered seeking asylum in Canada, but feared it would thwart his itinerant lifestyle. Every year, he attended book, film and music festivals across the globe. He could not do so whilst awaiting a decision on an asylum application: he would be confined to Canada. Processing asylum applications could take years, perhaps even a decade. Restriction to one country would be intolerable for a man who lived as though he had too much to do in extremely limited time. It was one thing to stay away from Nigeria, but another to be cooped up in another country, in a seemingly interminable wait for the grant of residency status.

Soon, however, a better door opened for him. The Department of English at the University of Johannesburg (UJ) offered him a Research Fellow position. The Head of Department, Prof. Sikhumbuzo Mngadi, who had watched his documentary on Flora Nwapa, was enthralled by it. He felt Onyeka could boost the scholarship on Nwapa and her works. I went to the Professor's office to collect the hardcopy letter of invitation on Onyeka's behalf. This happened in April 2019, when Onyeka was retrieving his International Passport from the Police Authorities at Alagbon, Lagos. He flew off to South Africa shortly afterwards.

Onyeka Nwelue and the author, at the University of Johannesburg, SA.

'I never thought I'd be saying something like this,' he told me, in our last face-to-face conversation before this publication. 'Thank you, South Africa. I never thought I'd be saying this, but thank you, Mandela's country, for being a solution to my mental health!' I leaned in my seat and just listened while he continued. 'I once told a policeman trying to drag me into a prison cell that I had depression, and he told me that if I accepted Jesus as my Lord and personal Savior, my depression would go away. God! If I hadn't left Nigeria, I'm sure by now I'd have become unhinged, roaming the streets, a raving lunatic.' I clenched my teeth, cleaving the laughter in the trenches of my gum, even as I could tell how right he was. Truly, if he had not left, he would have returned to prison repeatedly. If his incarceration was not caused by his creditors, it might be caused by the government. In Nigeria, opinionated journalists, voluble thinkers and activists, indeed any loquacious rabble-rouser was an endangered species. Knowing of Onyeka's blunt and unhesitating attacks or insults upon so-called public authorities, it was never going to be long before he was picked up and locked away like many others. Such incarceration would be fatal for someone in such a precarious mental state as he. It was perhaps to his ultimate advantage that Facebook administrators took down his Facebook Account and Page. It would have been impossible for him not to condemn and offend political authorities in Nigeria, most of whom are adept at tracking and 'dealing with' critics and perceived enemies.

Should I psychologize, however briefly, I would say that had Onyeka been given a chance to act differently, he would not have accepted it. I doubt that he would wish to change much about the manner in which he has lived so far. He would have regrets, which is common to all men. However, he would pursue every dream with the same tenacity. He would be the same impulsive and daring soul, the teenager who dropped out of an anthropology degree programme because he was sick of school. He would opt to remain the 16-year-old who boarded a night bus from Owerri to Lagos in order to see Soyinka in the flesh. He would still be the young man that took loans to finance his creative projects, without properly considering the consequences of defaulting over the refunds. He would not have shrunk from the many and fiery controversies of his 20s, nor would he have retracted his assessment of Achebe's *Things Fall Apart* as a mediocre novel.

I imagine that he would not wish to relive his weeklong incarceration in Rwanda, when his physical and mental health declined so fast that his jailers feared he might die. He might not have lashed out at Rwanda Air, and called Rwandans thieves after the theft of his cherished possessions on their flight. He would wish never to have been an inmate of Nigerian police cells in Lagos, Abuja and Benin. He would wish not to have suffered the trauma which each stint in custody inflicted on him. Time however, always goes forward, and life never goes backwards.

As we sat in his sitting room reflecting on these events, Onyeka remarked: 'I like my life like this. It may seem uneventful and quiet, but it is better. I don't have to carry anyone's burden anymore. People can only reach me via e-mail. And I decide whom I wish to speak or respond to.' When I surveyed his living space, it was evident that his life was not as tempestuous as it used to be. On the table were various pills, scattered like seeds on a Ludo board. One of them, he said, could slow down his brain. 'I never thought such medicine existed,' he noted, his face sober as a doctor's stitching a wound. 'When I take it, it feels as though it numbs my ability to muster the effort for thought. With that, it keeps me from all the thoughts that rob me of peace. I like it.'

His apartment is on the fourth floor of a massive high-rise, and the sitting room opens to a balcony at the back. It overlooks his workplace, the University of Johannesburg, and outer parts of the Maboneng Precinct. He told me he stood there most evenings, gazing at the city lights in the distance, as his incense burned alongside his coloured candles. There was a wine-rack loaded with red and sparkling wines that stood beside the towering refrigerator in the room. Next to it was a 60-inch television that appeared permanently tuned to the Netflix App. Before every wall in the room stood a bookshelf, each so heavily stacked that I could tell he had resumed his voracious reading. I recall moving to each shelf, peering at each spine, titillated whenever I saw a book I had read. One of the shelves was detached from the rest, and bore only two books: *My Watch 1, 2 &3* by Olusegun Obasanjo, and *The Thabo Mbeki I know* by Sifiso Mxolisi Ndlovu and Miranda Strydom. 'Why are these ones separated from the rest?' I asked. 'They were signed for me by the Presidents themselves,' he replied, his face radiant with satisfaction. I have seen that smile on many occasions. It is the smile of one who retains a rocklike faith in his own greatness, whether the world chooses to see it or not.

EPILOGUE

EZEOKE TO OXFORD

I wrote the final chapter of this book for over a year before I came to add an epilogue. For some reason, we (Onyeka and I) did not feel the impulse to publish the work back then. We couldn't tell what held us back, but neither of us felt it was time. There was just an unstated telepathy, a recognition from both of us that there was one more twist in the plot before we go to press. But what exactly that was, neither of us could tell. Thus, on that August morning when he shared his letter of appointment at the University of Oxford, I said, 'Well, what news! Maybe this was whom we've been waiting for.'

Onyeka's appointment was a pleasant shock for those of us close to him, and to an extent, himself as well. 'I feel like an imposter,' he told me, as we sat in a Korean restaurant somewhere in Sandton, Johannesburg. 'I am just as surprised too, to be frank, but very few things about you surprises me these days.' For a person who've dedicated himself to creative pursuits the way Onyeka has done since he was sixteen, I was sure these sorts of pinnacles were in his horizon; and I couldn't be more pleased to see his flowers arriving. Moreover, now that he was on his way to Oxford, I was upbeat for what the future held. It was in Onyeka's nature to create high value with any opportunity he gets, so that in no distant time, his opportunity becomes an opportunity for others. And that was exactly what happened.

Not long after Onyeka's move to Oxford, he set up The James Currey Society, which now partners with the African Studies Centre at the University of Oxford. Through that body, he's invited variegated personalities. People from the older generation like Professors Leslie Obiora and Akachi Ezigbo. Young Africans like Stephen Embleton, who was the runner up for the James Currey Prize for African Literature and the first James Currey Fellow at Oxford University. The James Currey Prize itself was set up in the early months of the coronavirus pandemic in 2020 and managed by a company co-founded by Onyeka and me and a young South African lady, Mmamello Matake. Media entrepreneurs like Linda Ikeji and Chude Jideonwo have both arrived to speak to guests at the African Studies Centre. And a lot of more people are on their way. This is something Onyeka does so well, and something he has done all his life. It was how we also met. His urgency to emboss whatever talents others have; to see that talent being expressed and shared as much as possible.

Knowing the travails of his life as discussed in the course of this work, one may wonder, how is Onyeka now and what's life like for him? Of course, this would always be a tough one to answer or predict given life's turns and the permanence of its impermanence. What I know now is that he is happier than he's ever been. Given how many times he said to me, 'Nna, I'm at the number one academic establishment in the world,' on the day we had a celebratory drink, I felt that there was a new spirit within him. That his restlessness, the sense of urgency to start something new, to be about something bigger, that this aspirational tension would give way, however small, to a sense of fulfilment.

Since I knew him, this was the first time I would see him relaxed about his aspirations. Discuss his vision or ongoing pursuits with a considerable degree of assuredness and not the imperious urgency that had defined his pursuits in earlier years. Maybe, it has something to do with being at a place where your dreams arrive to you without stripping you of all energy. For example, Onyeka co-organized (with Sally Dunsmore) the Oxford/FT Book Festival of 2022, where he was also on a panel with Booker Prize-winning Nigerian author, Ben Okri. When I watched the proceedings of the event, my mind went back to a story he told me about Bayelsa Book and Arts Festival he organized in 2013. It had ended in a fiasco, with several writers piling on him for delivering a shabby show. According to Onyeka, these writers wanted to be treated like newborns and the festival was too under-resourced to guarantee that. Whatever the case, he was in Oxford now co-organizing one of the biggest literary events in the UK. This was typical of Onyeka and the peculiar manifestations of his dreams however long in the making they seem.

There is yet another example. When Igbo language was welcomed to the University of Oxford following Onyeka's intervention, many people would have thought it was a dream conceived after his move to England. The truth was that, that moment had been 5 years in the making. I could recall immediately our encounter with Lai Mohammed, Nigeria's Minister for Information and Culture in Abuja. I could recall Onyeka making the case the Nigeria's major languages should be taught across the world through the cultural sections of our embassies abroad. As one would expect, such discussions are often too mentally tasking for the average Nigerian politician, and frankly possesses little political utility for them, and so it went no where. Years later, Ikechukwu Umeonyirioha, whom Onyeka had brought to Oxford from China, was teaching Igbo language to British-born Nigerians and others who were interested. The dream Mr. Lai rejected would come true, eventually. Not necessarily as initially planned, but it came to be in some way or form. For Onyeka, dreams are not just dreams. They are a tireless drumming in his head. They are revenant that don't go away. He would go to anyone who would see the value of his vision, anyone whose collaboration can lead to that grand goal, but if all these fails, he would go it alone. It speaks of the power of purpose, drive and conviction, that only few can muster in this age.

As for what the future holds for 34-year-old Onyeka, I don't know and cannot tell. Even he cannot tell. What I can predict, however, is that he will be onto many other pursuits, relentlessly, because he never stops. These pursuits, it must be understood provides him an essential window of escape, occluding the misery of living. Since his battle with bipolar is now one that must follow him forever, these pursuits are the very scaffolding that provides some radiance into his existence, rendering more bearable what is a troubled life.

GALLERY

With Booker Prize-winning author, Arundhati Roy in Johannesburg, South Africa.

*With bestselling author, Shobhaa De and husband, Dilip De
at Jaipur Literature Festival.*

*With
Arundhati Roy
in her home in
Delhi, India.*

With Nobel Laureate, Wole Soyinka, in his home, filming The Onyeka Nwelue Show.

With Wole Soyinka in his office, during a private film screening.

*Autographing for Nobel Laureate, Wole Soyinka in
his home in Abeokuta, Nigeria.*

*With former Nigerian President Olusegun Obasanjo, in his
home in Abeokuta, Nigeria.*

With Zakes Mda, at Ohio University in Athens, Ohio.

BLUES & HILLS PICTURES in conjunction with GRAVEL ROAD DISTRIBUTORS (SOUTH AFRICA) presents
AGWAETITI
Obịụtọ
A FILM BY
ONYEKA NWELUE
DIRECTOR: ONYEKA NWELUE
EXECUTIVE PRODUCERS: ONYEKA NWELUE, AROYEJI 'E' IYINOLUWA & OSONDU AWARAKA
"A magnificent work of art."
- WOLE SOYINKA
Nominee:2018 AFRICA MOVIE ACADEMY AWARDS (AMAA)
Best First Feature Film by a Director
Ousmane Sembene Award for Best Film in an African Language
NOMINEE
OFFICIAL SELECTION 2018
OFFICIAL SELECTION
Woodpecker
2018
LIGHTS CAMERA AFRICA FILM FESTIVAL 2018
SELECTED
Lake International PanAfrican Film Festival

With musical duo, Ibeyi in Havana, Cuba.

With British historian, William Darylmple in Jaipur, India.

With Nigerian musician, Asa in Paris, France.

With British actor and model, Dudley O'Shaughnessy in London, UK.

*With Jane Elliot in her home in California,
United States of America.*

With Chimamanda Ngozi Adichie in Lagos, Nigeria.

With South African activist, Denis Goldberg in Lagos, Nigeria.

With British publisher, James Currey in Accra, Ghana.

GLOSSARY

Olokpa	Police
Nna m	literally 'my father' but an affectionate term for male associates.
Okwa ihuru nwa ma ihe?	You see he is a sensible child?
Shurrup	Shut up
Jor	Slang used for humorous emphasis
Nyash	Buttocks
DSS	Directorate of State Security
Abobakus	A serf who is buried with their master
Babariga	A large flowing robe
Enyi gi nwanyi kwa nu?"	What about your girlfriend?

Emele nu ihe a nu, biko nu?	Don't do that, please
Onye a ogbagokwaranu ebe ahu g'ime gini	What did he climb up there to do?
I no dey house o!'	literally, 'I'm not at home!' with 'o' for emphasis. Expression of disinclination to talk.
gakwa gbara ogwu ha nuo o	Figuratively, 'Mind your business' with 'o' for emphasis.
Nna, ike agwula m."	Nna, I am weary/exhausted or 'I've had enough'
koboko	cowhide whip
Nne m	literally, 'my mother.' Used for females.
ogbu-oja	Flutist
Nna, jisie ike	Don't relent